Essential Education
Learning Made CERTAIN

Essential Writing Skills

Practice for Extended Response Writing

Authors

Maya Moore

Teresa Perrin

Jenni Romano

Nancy Schnog

Senior Consultants

Bonnie Goonen

Susan Pittman-Shetler

Published by Essential Education

Essential Writing Skills

ISBN 978-1-940532-04-2

For more information, contact:
Essential Education Corporation
895 NW Grant Avenue
Corvallis, OR 97330
phone: 800-931-8069

Cover Design: Karen Guard

Essential Education provides innovative, effective HSE test preparation and
adult learning programs centered on the learner's needs.
For more information, please visit http://www.passGED.com/educators/.

Table of Contents

Essential Education
Learning Made CERTAIN

Introduction

The *Essential Writing Skills* workbook will give you a foundation in planning, drafting, and finalizing writing. Your purpose in writing will vary, from passing a standardized test to applying for a job to writing a report or paper. Good writing skills will help you succeed in all types of writing tasks. Through this workbook, you'll learn to develop what you want to say and to express it clearly. After all, that's the purpose of writing—to develop and communicate ideas.

One important area of writing is analyzing and evaluating what you read. In the workplace, you will need to not only understand reports but read them with a critical eye. Discerning the best contracting bid or product description is an essential skill. In higher education, you will need to write original papers that reference and evaluate books, research papers, and other works. This workbook will give you practice writing about what you read.

As you practice writing, you will develop a good writing process:

- **Plan:** Read, research, brainstorm, and identify your central idea.

- **Draft:** Outline and write an introduction, body, and conclusion.

- **Evaluate:** Throughout the writing process, evaluate your work. As you evaluate, continue to plan, revise, and edit your draft.

- **Submit:** When your writing is done, proofread, format, and publish your work.

A writing process will give you a structure to develop your ideas around a strong central idea, to make decisions about organization and language, and to edit and finalize your work.

This writing book contains practice problems that involve several levels of knowledge and thinking:

⭐ If an exercise has one star, it is testing your ability to recall and use specific skills, such as grammar and language use.

⭐⭐ If an exercise has two stars, it asks you to interpret, summarize, or do other tasks that require some analysis. A two-star problem is checking to see if you have acquired a skill or concept.

⭐⭐⭐ If an exercise has three stars, it asks you to think strategically to answer a question or respond to a prompt. These exercises will require short or extended responses.

Technology Tip

As your writing improves, practice using a keyboard. Set a goal to type 20 to 50 words per minute.

You can use this workbook on its own, by working through each section, to improve your writing skills. The practice in this workbook will reinforce the skills you already have and develop new ones. You'll learn by applying those skills to many different situations. Practice helps you improve quickly because you're actively using the skills you're learning.

This workbook is also a good supplement to classroom learning or online courses, including Essential Education courses such as GED Academy™ and Essential Skills Online. You don't need to go through the workbook in one particular order. Instead, use whatever section teaches the skills you're currently learning. If you're in a class, your teacher can help you choose the best sections to study.

Take your time working through the exercises in this book. They're meant to enhance your thinking skills and to give you practice with many writing tasks, so that you can develop strong writing for any situation. If your writing speed is slow, work to increase your speed as you work through the book. Check Your Skills short answers and extended responses include target times for each exercise.

The Writing Process

Developing a strong writing process is the key to improving your writing. The writing process helps you develop content and focus on what you want to say. Good organization, specific details, and a strong central idea all come from using the writing process to plan, draft, and evaluate your writing. The steps of planning, drafting, and evaluating are not strict chronological steps. You will return to planning and drafting as you evaluate your writing.

There are many types of writing, from work reports to advertising to song lyrics to letters. You will approach a short task, such as an email, differently from a lengthy research paper. In both cases, you will plan, draft, and evaluate before you finalize what you've written and hit "send" or "print."

 Plan

Planning is the first step of the writing process, but you will return to planning as you draft and evaluate your work. Planning includes research, reading, developing a central idea, brainstorming, and organizing your ideas.

 Draft

Drafting doesn't happen all at once. Developing an outline and organizing your ideas makes writing your draft easier.

 Evaluate

Evaluating, revising, and editing can be a long task or a short one, depending on your writing task. Evaluate as you plan and draft, and based on your evaluation, revise and edit your work.

Submit

When you are satisfied with what you've written, it's time to finalize it. Review your work one last time to catch minor errors. You might need to format a paper, put the bibliography in the proper format, print your final draft, and turn it in to your instructor.

The writing process is critical for formal writing tasks: college entrance essays, college papers, exams, work reports, documentation, and memos. No matter what writing task you approach, the writing process will help you find something meaningful to say and express it well.

Plan, Draft, Evaluate

Connections

Have you ever...

- Had no idea how to start a writing assignment?
- Written an important email to a supervisor or client?
- Composed a letter to your senator or representative?

Writing isn't just churning out words. To write successfully, you use a **process**. Whether you are emailing a client to describe company policies, writing a New Year's message to all your family, or composing a research paper for a college class, writing involves making many decisions. You choose your length, topic, words, and tone. All of those decisions affect your message and your reader.

Consciously following a writing process helps you make deliberate choices to write effectively. Use a four-step writing process to improve your writing:

 Plan: Examine your task. Who is the audience? What is the purpose? Research your topic, read and examine source materials, brainstorm ideas, and think through what you want to say.

The Writing Process

 Draft: Prewrite and compose your work. You might start with a central idea, some supporting ideas, and evidence or examples. Then, fill in details, connections, transitions, and conclusions.

 Evaluate: As you work, evaluate your writing. Is it successful? Does it communicate? Continue to plan, revise, and edit your draft.

Submit **Submit:** When your work is ready, make final changes and publish. That might mean posting your work on your blog, submitting a paper to your professor, or mailing a letter to a company.

Use the first three steps together. As you plan, prewrite and evaluate. As you draft, plan and evaluate. As you evaluate, plan, rewrite, and edit.

Plan, Draft, and Evaluate Your Writing

The writing process helps you approach writing thoughtfully so you can improve your skills. You will make conscious decisions through planning and revising.

Imagine you need to make a recommendation to your boss about which printer to purchase for the office. You work in a busy office that prints up to 1,000 pages per day. Examine the table and write a recommendation, including your reasoning.

	Price	Speed (Pages per Minute)	Monthly Workload	Ink Cost (Cents per Page)
Printer A	$459	24 ppm	70,000 pages	4.2
Printer B	$624	28 ppm	50,000 pages	2.3

Plan

First, examine your task. What is your purpose? Who is your audience? Is this a formal or informal task? What do you need to read and understand? What do you want to say? Strategies that help you think through writing tasks and plan your writing include:

- Defining purpose and audience

- Brainstorming

- Researching

Writing doesn't occur in a vacuum. Developing good ideas and strong content depends on reading and investigating as well as thinking and prewriting.

 1. Determine which printer to recommend. Give two reasons why.

> *Technology Tip*
>
> If you are working on a computer, keep a copy of your prewriting as you write so you don't lose your ideas.

You might recommend Printer B. Although it is more expensive, it will cost 1.9 cents less per page in ink. If you print 1,000 pages a day, that's $20 per day. Printer B is also slightly faster.

Draft

When you start writing, you won't usually just sit down and begin composing sentences. Especially if you're writing a large project, start by organizing your ideas. First, develop a structure or outline, and fill in some important details and ideas. Then, complete your draft. Even a short project will have a beginning, a middle, and an ending.

? **2.** Draft a full paragraph, with a beginning, middle, and ending, recommending a printer.

You might write:

> I recommend Printer B because it will be more cost effective. Printer A costs approximately $175 less than Printer B, but Printer B has an ink cost of 1.9 cents per page less than Printer A. At 1,000 pages per day, the savings in ink will be approximately $20 per day. It will take less than two weeks to recoup the extra cost of Printer B. Workload and print speed are minor factors. Both printers can handle our monthly workload (about 30,000 pages) equally well, but Printer B has a slightly faster print speed. Printer B is clearly the best choice based on the available data.

Notice that this paragraph has a beginning (stating the recommendation), a middle (giving specific evidence), and an ending (summing up the recommendation).

 Evaluate

All writing can be improved. During and after writing, evaluate your work and make changes.

- **Read critically:** Approach your text with fresh eyes to improve it.
- **Revise:** Make changes to organization, tone, and content.
- **Edit:** Reorganize, improve language, and clear up confusing passages.

? **3.** Review your paragraph, and make revisions to improve it.

You might clarify ideas, improve the organization, or add details.

Submit

When you are satisfied that your writing is ready, proofread to make any final corrections and format your work in its final form. Then publish your work—send your email or letter, submit your paper, or post your blog entry.

? **4.** Proofread your paragraph and make any final corrections.

Make a note of common errors in your writing to help you catch mistakes when you proofread. In an office, the final step would be to send or give your recommendation to your boss.

Use your understanding of the writing process to complete the following exercises.

 1. Sharon needs to write a paper about the history of ranching in her state. How can she plan before she begins to write?

 2. Andrew has been assigned to write an essay about Congress for a civics class. How can he decide on a more specific topic?

 3. Ralph is writing a report for work to analyze productivity in his department.

    a. What does Ralph need to think about before he begins writing?

    b. How can Ralph approach writing the report to keep it organized?

    c. How can Ralph evaluate his writing?

 4. Mauricio intends to write about nuclear-powered submarines for a science paper. He has made a list of information he knows about submarines and has found three books about how they function.

    a. Where is Mauricio in the writing process?

    b. What advice would you give to Mauricio to proceed?

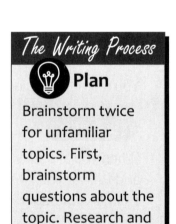

The Writing Process

Plan

Brainstorm twice for unfamiliar topics. First, brainstorm questions about the topic. Research and then brainstorm again, including ideas and more questions.

Use the following passage for exercise 5.

Solar flares have a direct effect on the Earth's atmosphere. The intense radiation from a solar flare travels to Earth in eight minutes. As a result the Earth's upper atmosphere becomes more ionized and expands. Long-distance radio signals can be disrupted by the resulting change in the Earth's ionosphere. A satellite's orbit around the Earth can be disturbed by the enhanced drag on the satellite from the expanded atmosphere, and satellites' electronic components can be damaged.

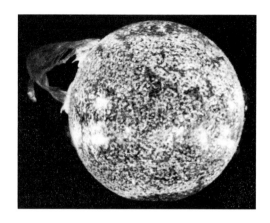

Source: Adapted from "Why Study Solar Flares?" at The Solar Flare Theory Educational Web Pages by NASA's Goddard Space Flight Center. http://hesperia.gsfc.nasa.gov/sftheory/studyflare.htm

 5. Explain possible advantages of being able to predict solar flares.

  a. **Plan:** What is the purpose and audience? What will you write?

  b. **Draft:** Draft a paragraph to fulfill this writing task.

  c. **Evaluate and Submit:** Evaluate your paragraph to revise and edit it.

6. How does revising your work as you evaluate it differ from proofreading work that you are finalizing?

Use the following letter to the editor for exercise 7.

I strongly disagree with last Sunday's editorial against the city's plan to close the Bradley Branch Library. Libraries do have valuable services, but they are being replaced by services available over the Internet. Is the Bradley Library bustling with readers every day? I doubt it, otherwise the city would not choose to close it. It is natural that, when you can download unlimited ebooks from the Internet and browse unlimited websites, our city should reduce its number of libraries. Patrons can travel a little further to another branch.

 7. Critique the argument in this letter to the editor. Is the reasoning sound? What are possible counterarguments?

    a. 💡 **Plan:** What is the purpose and audience? What will you write?

    b. ✏️ **Draft:** Draft a paragraph to fulfill this writing task.

    c. ⚙️ **Evaluate and** (**Submit**): Evaluate your paragraph and revise it.

8. Imagine that you are planning to write a blog post to share a recipe. How would you use the writing process?

Check **Your Skills**

Use the writing process to write short responses to the following exercises.

 1. Lee is writing a blog post describing how to build a shed. He begins to draft his post. Two paragraphs later, after describing the steps, he runs out of things to say. His post seems too short, and he's not sure what to do. Describe how Lee can use the writing process to improve his writing and revise his blog post.

Write your answer below or type your response on a computer. Take approximately 25 minutes to respond.

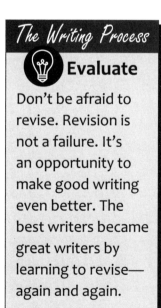

The Writing Process

Evaluate

Don't be afraid to revise. Revision is not a failure. It's an opportunity to make good writing even better. The best writers became great writers by learning to revise— again and again.

Use the questions on page 99 to evaluate your response.

The following passage is from the book *Are Women People?* by Alice Duer Miller. The book is a collection of short passages and poetry in support of giving women the right to vote.

Use the following passage for exercise 2.

The Logic of the Law

In 1875 the Supreme Court of Wisconsin in denying the petition of women to practise before it said: "It would be shocking to man's reverence for womanhood and faith in woman ... that woman should be permitted to mix professionally in all the nastiness which finds its way into courts of justice."

It then names thirteen subjects as unfit for the attention of women—three of them are crimes committed against women.

Source: From *Are Women People?* by Alice Duer Miller, 1915.

 2. Explain and critique this passage as an argument that women should be allowed to argue cases before courts. Write your answer below or type your response on a computer. Take approximately 25 minutes to respond.

Remember the Concept

Plan, Draft, Evaluate before you submit.

The Writing Process

Submit

Use the questions on page 99 to evaluate your response.

Organization

Organization is one of the most important elements of good writing. Developing well-organized writing will also help you have a strong central idea, specific supporting details, and a compelling conclusion. Good organization helps you communicate well.

*   You need a clear central idea so that you can develop an organization that supports your idea.

*   You need strong evidence to show a logical progression of ideas and support your central idea.

*   You need to explain your evidence and why it supports your central idea.

*   You need a good conclusion to give your writing a satisfying ending.

The most basic elements of organization are a beginning, middle, and ending. Every paragraph, letter, email, paper, report, blog post, poem, or book you might write has a beginning, middle, and ending.

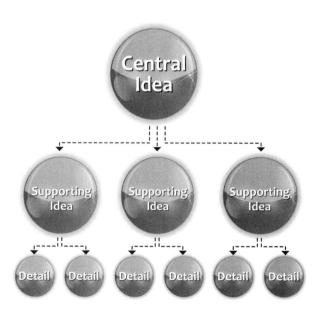

The beginning introduces your ideas. Like the first few minutes of a movie or book, it catches the reader's attention and sets up what will follow. What is your tone? What is your position? In a paper or academic response, the introduction should include a statement of your central idea: your thesis. Give any background or details that help you explain and set up your central idea.

The middle is the main part of your writing. The middle contains the support for your central idea and explains your thinking. It is the longest part and often the most difficult. To be successful writing the middle, you need to develop good content. That means identifying enough supporting ideas and specific details to accomplish the goal of your writing task. Explain the connections between your ideas, and present them in a logical order.

The ending is your last chance to communicate with the reader. To leave your reader with a positive impression, you want a strong ending, or conclusion. Just like a bad ending can ruin a movie, a bad ending can leave a paper or academic response flat. The best conclusions give some new insight into the ideas the author presents, while restating the central idea in a new way. How does the central idea apply to a bigger picture? What is an unaddressed point or unanswered question?

This section will give you additional practice developing your organization for specific situations.

- **Organizing Short Answers**
  Apply techniques for organization to paragraph-length responses.

- **Organizing Extended Responses**
  Develop a good organization for longer academic and workplace responses.

Organizing Short Answers

Connections

Have you ever...

- Responded to a post on a blog?

- Described a process or event to a new hire?

- Decided how to reply to an email from a client?

Each of these tasks requires a short response. A short response is brief, but it still needs to be organized. If you're reading a recipe, you want clear directions. If you're reading an email, you want to understand the main point. When you write, organization helps you communicate clearly.

Short answers require analyzing an issue or question and then providing a brief but effective answer or comment in an appropriate tone. Because the response is shorter, every sentence should add to the meaning, purpose, and clarity of your communication.

A short answer typically replies to a question, prompt, or passage. In a college class or formal exam, you will have to write short answers to show your knowledge, typically in a limited time frame. With limited time, organization is especially important. Plan, draft, and evaluate to organize your writing.

- **Plan** a central idea and supporting details by examining materials and thinking through the task.

- **Draft** a well-organized response focused on your central idea.

- **Evaluate** whether the organization of your response communicates clearly and effectively.

Organizing a Short Answer Using the Writing Process

You should be able to write an effective short answer in about ten minutes. Your response should be a full, complete paragraph with a beginning, middle, and ending. The key to good organization in a short response is to have a developed central idea with supporting details.

Read the following passage. Explain how the data from water samples supports or does not support the conclusion that *E. coli* bacteria levels are not affected by temperature or pH levels. Include multiple pieces of evidence from the passage to support your answer. Take approximately 10 minutes to respond.

Little Creek *E. coli* Bacteria Study

The Little Creek *E. coli* Bacteria Study is an effort to determine the source or sources of elevated *E. coli* levels in Little Creek, an important component of our city's watershed and a popular swimming hole during the summer months. Effects of ingesting *E. coli* include severe abdominal cramping, diarrhea, and seizures, but Little Creek's *E. coli* levels are within acceptable levels for recreation.

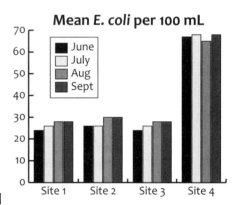

In June, July, August, and September, scientists measured temperature, pH, and levels of *E. coli* at four sites. The goal of the study was to learn whether temperature or pH were factors in raised levels of *E. coli*. Temperature was measured in degrees Fahrenheit. Warmer temperatures can encourage bacterial growth. The pH levels show acidity or basicity of the water. A pH level of less than seven signals basicity, a more ideal environment for bacteria growth.

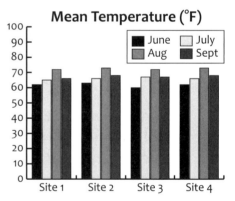

Results indicate that neither temperature nor pH levels have triggered the high levels of *E. coli*. Water temperatures are expectedly higher in the hotter months of July and August, but *E. coli* levels during those months remain the same regardless of water temperature. Nor does the data point to pH levels as a cause of *E. coli*.

However, increased levels of *E. coli* were found at Site 4, the location where water from a farm irrigation ditch (FID) is released into Little Creek. The FID is uncovered and therefore an open target for chemical farm runoff, animal feces, and other toxins.

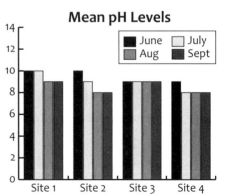

Plan

Focus on organization right away for a short answer. Examine the question and source materials. Identify two things:

- What is your central idea?

- What are supporting details?

Your central idea and details will drive the organization of your response.

? **1.** Write a one-sentence central idea, and identify two to four details from the passage to support the central idea.

The exercise is asking you to show how the claim made in the report is either supported or not supported by the data. You will need to study the data in the charts and determine whether the claim made in the report is supported by this data. Since the data supports the claim, you might write:

> In the Little Creek *E. coli* Bacteria Study, the claim that *E. coli* levels are not affected by temperature or pH levels is supported by the data.

Since you examined the data to come to this conclusion, you should be able to identify details to support it:

> Levels of *E. coli* do not go up when the temperature rises in the hotter months of July and August. Site 2 is a good example.

> The pH levels do not drop below seven, which would create an environment to encourage bacterial growth.

> Site 4 has similar temperature and pH as other sites, but it has more bacteria.

Draft

A short answer is typically one full paragraph. Organize your paragraph:

- Start with the central idea at the beginning.

- Fill the middle with details. Add specifics from the passage and make connections to the central idea.

- Add a conclusion at the end.

? **2.** Draft your response as a full paragraph using the following organizer.

Beginning:	*Your Central Idea*

Middle:	*Supporting Details and Connection to the Central Idea*

Ending:	*Conclusion*

Your response might look like this:

> In the Little Creek *E. coli* Bacteria Study, the claim that *E. coli* levels are not affected by temperature or pH levels is supported by the data. The chart shows that levels of *E. coli* did not go up when the temperature rose in the hotter months of July and August. For example, at Site 2, the *E. coli* level was the same in June and July, while

temperatures rose from the low to high 60s. The bacteria level rose in August, but stayed the same in September, although temperatures fell. Since high temperatures encourage bacterial growth, you might expect high temperature to correlate with higher bacterial levels. Since this wasn't the case, something else must have caused high levels of bacteria. There was a similar lack of correlation between pH and *E. coli*, according to the data. The pH never dropped below seven, a pH level that might encourage bacterial growth. Site 4 had high *E. coli* levels, but the pH remained at 8 or 9. The pH and temperature at Site 4 were the same as or less than the other sites, but the bacteria level was consistently higher. Since the data shows that high *E. coli* levels were not caused by temperature or pH, they must have been caused by something else. The passage suggests that they were caused by runoff from a farm, which would be a good avenue for further study.

 ## *Evaluate and Submit*

Evaluate your organization as you draft. Does it make sense? Do you need transitions, more specific details, or connections to the central idea? Make changes to clarify your ideas and improve your organization. Continue to evaluate after you draft, until you are ready to submit your response.

? **3.** Revise your short answer to improve its organization.

Since you often have limited time to write a short response, evaluate as you plan and draft. When you're finished, do one last check for language errors, clarity, and transitions.

Practice It!

In a scientific study, a control group is a group that is not affected by the factor being studied. For example, in a study of how constant, strong light affects plant growth, a control group might receive normal light. This allows scientists to compare the experimental group, which has undergone a treatment, to the control group, which has received no treatment, in order to more effectively test for an independent variable. Using a control group is especially necessary when there are complex factors that might affect the experiment. Administering a placebo is one example of using a control group. While one group receives a dose of medication, the other group receives a "fake dose," meant to have no effect. In this way, the experiment can account for complex factors—for example a flu that is going around or the body's natural ability to heal on its own—that might affect the experiment.

1. Explain how a control group could be used for a study on the effect of regular exercise on clinical depression. Discuss the importance of the control group for the larger study. Include multiple pieces of evidence from the passage to support your answer.

   a. Write a one-sentence central idea and identify two to four details from the passage to support the central idea.

The Writing Process

Draft

Use specific details and connect them to your central idea.

b. Draft your response as a full paragraph. Evaluate as you draft and after you draft.

Beginning: *Your Central Idea*

Middle: *Supporting Details and Connection to the Central Idea*

Ending: *Conclusion*

Use the following passage from an employee handbook for exercise 2.

Doscero Industries encourages an open environment where employees can voice their ideas and concerns. We believe that free communication leads to improvement of our processes and policies and prevents negative behavior on a systemic level. If an employee has a concern about ethics, that concern should be voiced to the employee's manager. Managers are responsible for maintaining a supportive environment for free communication of all concerns. If a concern involves the manager's performance directly, the employee should voice this concern to the manager's superior. Any reported instance of potentially unethical or questionable behaviors or policies will be investigated thoroughly. The company will act promptly to respond to improper behavior and will not tolerate any retaliation against employees who raise their concerns in good faith.

 2. Kara works for Doscero Industries. She notices that her manager distributes less work to his good friend, Kara's coworker Max. Explain what actions you would recommend Kara take based on the company policy. Include multiple pieces of evidence from the passage to support your answer.

    a. Write a one-sentence central idea and identify two to four details from the passage to support the central idea.

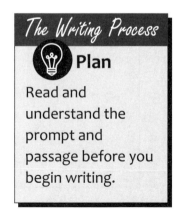

The Writing Process

Plan

Read and understand the prompt and passage before you begin writing.

b. Draft your response as a full paragraph. Evaluate as you draft and after you draft.

Beginning:	*Your Central Idea*

Middle:	*Supporting Details and Connection to the Central Idea*

Ending:	*Conclusion*

Check Your Skills

Use the following passage to write well-organized responses for exercises 1 and 2.

Amplified Greenhouse Effect Shifts North's Growing Seasons

Vegetation growth at Earth's northern latitudes increasingly resembles lusher latitudes to the south, according to a NASA-funded study based on a 30-year record of ground-based and satellite data sets.

"Higher northern latitudes are getting warmer. Arctic sea ice and the duration of snow cover are diminishing. The growing season is getting longer, and plants are growing more," said Ranga Myneni of Boston University's Department of Earth and Environment.

An amplified greenhouse effect is driving the changes, according to Myneni. Increased concentrations of heat-trapping gasses, such as water vapor, carbon dioxide, and methane, cause Earth's surface, ocean, and lower atmosphere to warm. Warming reduces the extent of polar sea ice and snow cover, and, in turn, the darker ocean and land surfaces absorb more solar energy, thus further heating the air above them.

"This sets in motion a cycle of positive reinforcement between warming and loss of sea ice and snow cover, which we call the amplified greenhouse effect," Myneni said. "The greenhouse effect could be further amplified in the future as soils in the north thaw, releasing potentially significant amounts of carbon dioxide and methane."

However, researchers note that plant growth in the north may not continue on its current trajectory. The ramifications of an amplified greenhouse effect, such as frequent forest fires, outbreaks of pest infestations, and summertime droughts, may slow plant growth. Also, warmer temperatures alone in the boreal zone do not guarantee more plant growth, which also depends on the availability of water and sunlight.

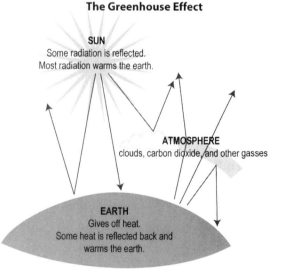

Source: Adapted from "Amplified Greenhouse Effect Shifts North's Growing Seasons." Author: Kathryn Hansen. Production editor: Dr. Tony Phillips. Credit: Science@NASA. http://science.nasa.gov/science-news/science-at-nasa/2013/10mar_greenhouseshift/

Organizing Short Answers

 1. Describe and evaluate the arguments given in the article for why the amplified greenhouse effect may not mean a continued increase in plant growth in the northern latitudes at the present rate. Include multiple pieces of evidence from the passage to support your answer.

Write your answer below, or type your response on a computer. Take approximately 10 minutes to respond.

 2. The greenhouse effect is projected to cause ice melt in the arctic and antarctic. Explain how the greenhouse effect would cause arctic and antarctic ice to melt. Include multiple pieces of evidence from the passage to support your answer.

Write your answer below, or type your response on a computer. Take approximately 10 minutes to respond.

Technology Tip

When you write on a computer, you can write your central idea and details as a brief outline. Then fill in the connections, more details, and conclusions.

Use the questions on page 99 to evaluate your response.

25

Use the following passage to write a well-organized response for exercise 3.

A U.S. Senator has proposed a bill that would cut military spending by 10% over the next five years. Those supporting the bill argue that military spending of over $670 billion a year is unnecessary and unreasonable when Russia and China combined spend only around $150 billion annually on their militaries. Those arguing against the bill state that it is dangerous to national security to cut military spending. They point out that the Department of Defence budget is only approximately 17% of the U.S. budget and encourage budget cuts in other areas, especially the Department of Health and Human Services (including Medicare and Medicaid) and the Social Security Administration, which together total over 47% of the budget.

3. Write a short email to your U.S. Senator, explaining either your support for or opposition to the bill described in the passage. Include multiple pieces of evidence from the passage to support your answer.

Write your answer below or type your response on a computer. Take approximately 10 minutes to respond.

Remember the Concept

Plan: Identify a central idea and supporting details.

Draft: Organize a paragraph with a beginning, middle, and ending.

Evaluate: Evaluate your organization as your write.

Use the questions on page 99 to evaluate your response.

Organizing Extended Responses

Connections

Have you ever...

- Defended a decision you made for your company?

- Expressed your views about a local issue for your school?

- Analyzed news articles about a political controversy?

Good organization will help you communicate well about complex topics. At work or in college, you will need to write responses to reports, books, or memos. Many careers and degrees require independent research to investigate topics. In your personal life, you may need to respond to a letter from a company, write a blog post reviewing a movie, or exchange emails about a political issue.

In an **extended response** you analyze written material and present your ideas backed by evidence. On an exam, your time will often be limited. The writing process will help you evaluate the issue, gather evidence, formulate your conclusion, and organize your work.

Plan: Review materials, develop your central idea, find evidence, and begin organizing your ideas into an appropriate structure.

Draft: Write a response within a clear organizational structure, including an introduction, body, and conclusion.

Evaluate: Review your writing for clarity, sense, and transitions. Make sure your organization communicates well and is easy to follow.

Submit Make any final corrections, and submit your response.

An extended response should have good organization, well-developed ideas, and substantial details. Organization is essential to an effective response.

Developing an Organized Extended Response

A well-organized response has a clear beginning, middle, and ending. It contains supporting details clearly connected to the central idea. The organization is appropriate to the purpose, and there is a clear, logical progression of ideas.

Read the following passages and write an extended response in which you analyze both positions. Explain which position is best supported and why. Include multiple pieces of evidence from the passages to support your answer. Typing your response on a computer will give you the best practice. Your total writing time should be about 45 minutes.

Non-voters Are Not Participating in the Political Process

U.S. voter turnout has shrunk to abysmally low levels during the last three decades. In 1996, less than half the qualifying citizens bothered to cast votes for the President of the United States! After fighting to secure our independence and to obtain voting rights for minorities and women, it is a shame that our citizens have become so complacent. Folks, we are dropping the ball.

As the eminent philosopher John Stuart Mill said, "Political machinery does not act of itself. As it is first made, so it has to be worked, by men, and even by ordinary men. It needs, not their simple acquiescence, but their active participation." Voter participation is an example of active participation at the most fundamental level. It is the one act that every ordinary man can do. It happens only once or twice a year and does not require extensive traveling, public speaking engagements, or monetary investment. Without democratic participation, government fails. Our government doesn't simply keep running without maintenance and care. Wake up, non-voters! Without full voter participation our government is not complete, and we will continue to drop the ball.

Non-voting Is Action!

I am writing in response to the article accusing non-voters of "dropping the ball." This narrow perception is so far from the truth that I wonder if the author has any idea at all about the nature of today's political climate. Today's U.S. voters are presented with a two-party system that is so rigid and heavily enforced that other parties have little to no chance of ever presenting their views to the general public, much less getting elected.

The result is a large group of voters who choose not to vote as a means of expressing their distaste for the consistently limited choice of candidates. By choosing not to vote, the citizen is proclaiming, "I don't like either of them." While this may not seem like John Stuart Mill's idea of "active participation," it is the only voting-booth-related action available to citizens who refuse to choose the lesser of two evils. Rather than blame non-voters for "dropping the ball," let's look at our disenfranchising political system.

 Plan

If you have 45 minutes to write an extended response, it helps to come to the task prepared with an organizational structure in mind. The most common organizational structure for this type of writing is a Statement & Support structure. Start by using and learning the Statement & Support graphic organizer.

An extended response is dependent on material that you must understand and analyze. Spend about ten minutes of planning time purposefully reading. Identify important ideas, good or flawed arguments, and other details that will help you build a central idea.

? 1. Spend about 10 minutes filling out the graphic organizer with a central idea, supporting ideas, and evidence from the passages. You may expand the chart to include more supporting ideas.

Statement & Support

Central Idea:	Details or Explanation:
Supporting Idea:	Details and Evidence:
Supporting Idea:	Details and Evidence:
Conclusion:	Details or Explanation:

You might complete the organizer like this:

Central Idea:	Details or Explanation:
"Non-voters Are Not Participating in the Political Process" has a better argument.	Provides some facts and evidence, while the other is unsupported opinion.
Supporting Idea: "Not Participating" uses a logical argument that government doesn't work without voter participation and that it is not a huge task to vote.	**Details and Evidence:** "political machinery does not act of itself" Voting does affect government. "It happens only once or twice a year and does not require extensive traveling" True, though voting can sometimes be difficult.
Supporting Idea: "Non-voting Is Action!" lacks support	**Details and Evidence:** "other parties have little to no chance of … getting elected" is not always true "choose not to vote as a means of expressing their distaste" has no evidence. Is this really why?
Conclusion: The first is better supported but is calling people "complacent" helpful?	**Details or Explanation:** Voting can be made easier or mandated. Just calling people "complacent" doesn't help solve the problem.

Draft

Your draft should include a beginning, middle, and ending:

- **Beginning:** Introduce your ideas. Include an interesting beginning, your central idea, and any details or explanation you need to introduce your ideas. You don't need to list all your supporting ideas. That's not interesting, and it doesn't set up your ideas for the reader. In fact, it can cause repetition in your writing and a lack of fluidity.

- **Middle:** Explain each of your supporting ideas, using details and evidence. Connect each idea clearly to your central idea. Restate ideas from the passage instead of relying on direct quotes. If you do use a direct quote, explain its significance.

- **Ending:** Connect your ideas to a larger picture, or draw additional conclusions about your central idea. What makes your central idea meaningful? What did you discover in the process of planning and drafting? What additional thoughts do you have? Sum up your ideas, but be careful not to be redundant.

2. Spend about 20 minutes drafting your extended response on a computer or separate sheet of paper.

Evaluate

Evaluate your organization as you write and after you complete your draft.

- Do you have logical transitions between ideas?

- Do you make connections between your arguments and evidence?

- Do you have evidence and details to support your ideas?

- Do you have a strong central idea supported by the organization?

 3. Spend about 10 minutes evaluating your organization and revising your work.

Submit

Take a final look over your extended response to make any final corrections. Then, submit your response. Here is a sample response:

> Why do some citizens choose not to vote? Are they dissatisfied or complacent? The article "Non-voters Are Not Participating in the Political Process" claims that non-voters are "dropping the ball." It presents a stronger case than the rebuttal article, which attributes a specific attitude to non-voters with little evidence.
>
> The author of the "Not Participating" article makes a logical argument that voter participation is necessary for a government to function properly. He or she quotes John Stuart Mill that government does not run itself. Voting does affect government policies and actions. The author also argues that voting is not difficult since it happens seldom and since polling booths are near every neighborhood. Though the author supports his or her idea with facts, voting can sometimes be difficult for those with no transportation, no child care, or difficulty getting off work.
>
> The rebuttal article claims that people choose not to vote because they are dissatisfied with the lack of choices in the two-party system. It claims that not voting is a form of active participation. The article makes a valid point that the two-party system forces out alternative opinions, but it overstates the idea that other parties can't get elected. Third-party candidates are elected in local elections, as governors, and as congressmen. However, the author's main point is that people don't vote due to disgust with the two-party system, and the article fails to give any evidence to support this statement. Is political dissatisfaction really the reason non-voters don't visit the polls?
>
> In truth, there are likely many types of non-voters. Understanding their reasoning requires sociological study which is lacking in both opinion articles. Though the article opposing non-voters is stronger, scolding non-voters for "dropping the ball" accomplishes little. Examining ideas such as mandatory voting, early voting, and voting by mail is a better way to attack the problem of voter non-participation.

Practice It!

Use the following passages for exercise 1.

I am certainly not an advocate for frequent and untried changes in laws and constitutions. I think moderate imperfections had better be borne with; because, when once known, we accommodate ourselves to them, and find practical means of correcting their ill effects. But I know also, that laws and institutions must go hand in hand with the progress of the human mind. As that becomes more developed, more enlightened, as new discoveries are made, new truths disclosed, and manners and opinions change with the change of circumstances, institutions must advance also, and keep pace with the times. We might as well require a man to wear still the coat which fitted him when a boy, as civilized society to remain ever under the regimen of their barbarous ancestors.

—*Thomas Jefferson*

Source: Thomas Jefferson, Letter to Samuel Kercheval, June 12, 1816. Available at http://teachingamericanhistory.org/library/document/letter-to-samuel-kercheval/

The U.S. Supreme Court makes interpretations of our constitutional rights, but sometimes their interpretations are simply wrong. In its Citizens United ruling, the Court ruled that corporations as "associations of citizens" retain the right of free speech based on the First Amendment to the Constitution. Because of this ruling, corporations are allowed to spend unlimited amounts of money, often anonymously, to support politicians and political causes.

But free speech is a human right. Corporations are inhuman, legal entities without inherent rights. Corporations exist to protect their owners and officers from liability from their businesses. Should they then be considered "associations of citizens" with rights to free speech? Citizens can support candidates. Corporations are not citizens. They do not vote. They cannot be jailed. They are self-interested in laws that will help them make money. That is why I support a constitutional amendment declaring that corporations do not have constitutional rights.

—*Alphonse Kittridge*

1. In your response, develop an argument about how Mr. Kittridge's position reflects the enduring issue expressed in the excerpt from Thomas Jefferson. Analyze the strength of Mr. Kittridge's argument. Incorporate relevant and specific evidence from the passages and your own knowledge of the enduring issue and the circumstances to support your analysis. Type your response on a computer if possible or use a separate sheet of paper. Take up to 45 minutes to respond.

   a. **Plan:** Spend about 10 minutes filling out the graphic organizer with a central idea, supporting ideas, and evidence from the passages.

Statement & Support

Central Idea:	Details or Explanation:
Supporting Idea:	Details and Evidence:
Supporting Idea:	Details and Evidence:
Conclusion:	Details or Explanation:

   b. **Draft:** Spend about 20 minutes drafting your extended response on a computer or on a separate sheet of paper.

   c. **Evaluate and Submit:** Spend about 10 minutes evaluating your organization and revising your work before finalizing your extended response.

Use the following passage to complete exercise 2.

Zero-Tolerance Policies in Schools

Many schools have implemented "zero-tolerance" policies toward violence among students. These policies are often responses to school shootings and other extreme instances of school violence. Under zero-tolerance policies, any violence will result in suspension or expulsion. These polices have resulted in significant controversy.

The goal of zero-tolerance violence policies is to discourage violence by removing any violent students from the school. Proponents state that students cannot learn where there is the threat of violent behavior, and expelling all students who participate in violence is a strong deterrent. They argue that strong policies are needed in order to prevent disastrous violent events such as school shootings.

A zero-tolerance violence policy disallows students from making excuses and removes potentially biased administrative decisions based on conflicting reports from students, according to proponents. Even teacher reports can be unreliable, proponents say, since witness reports of what happened in violent situations is notoriously undependable. Zero-tolerance violence policies in schools discourage all violent behavior so that schools can maintain a safe environment for learning, proponents say.

However, zero-tolerance violence policies have come under criticism for their unconditional response to violent behavior. Students who are bullied or attacked must not defend themselves or they will face expulsion in many situations. In some instances, a student who is attacked is considered involved in a violent incident, whether or not he or she fights back.

Parents and students argue that expulsion is often unfair and unnecessary, and some parents object that they should have a say in the punishment of their sons and daughters. Instead of creating a violence-free, safe environment, opponents say, zero-tolerance policies create an insecure atmosphere where students fear they can be expelled by a twist of fate. Opponents are also concerned that expulsion does not deal with the problem of violent behavior; it merely removes violence from the school and pushes it into the community.

Debate over zero-tolerance violence policies continues as communities try to balance individual rights with the good of the school as a whole.

2. Read the passage, which gives arguments for and against zero-tolerance violence policies in school. In your response, analyze both positions to determine which one is best supported. Use specific evidence from the passage to support your claim. Take approximately 45 minutes to respond.

   a. **Plan:** Spend about 10 minutes filling out the graphic organizer with a central idea, supporting ideas, and evidence from the passages.

Statement & Support

Central Idea:	Details or Explanation:
Supporting Idea:	Details and Evidence:
Supporting Idea:	Details and Evidence:
Conclusion:	Details or Explanation:

   b. **Draft:** Spend about 20 minutes drafting your extended response on a computer or on a separate sheet of paper.

   c. **Evaluate and Submit:** Spend about 10 minutes evaluating your organization and revising your work before finalizing your extended response.

Check Your Skills

Use the following passage for exercises 1 and 2.

People use energy drinks to stay alert while driving, to stay up late and study, or as a morning or afternoon boost. These drinks cause an increase in energy often followed by a "crash." Energy drinks contain caffeine—sometimes as much as 184 milligrams—combined with sweeteners and other ingredients. Even if you've never been tempted to reach for an energy drink, you are probably familiar with the controversy over this relatively new addition to our beverage aisles.

Because of the extreme levels of caffeine and the resulting negative health effects, some consumers have proposed banning energy drinks or developing regulations to keep them away from children and expectant mothers. Proponents of a ban are especially concerned about the industry's penchant for marketing to children and teens, in some instances distributing free samples at youth sporting events.

In 2010, a high school football player in Missouri had a seizure and stopped breathing after consuming an energy drink. He now speaks against the use of energy drinks and works to get them removed from campuses. The symptoms that appear on the list of energy drink incidents documented by the Food and Drug Administration include convulsions, hypertension, loss of consciousness, anaphylactic shock, renal failure, and death. There have also been cases of fetal distress syndrome and miscarriages by pregnant women who consumed energy drinks.

Banning energy drinks or increasing regulation might seem to be in the public interest. However, companies are quick to point out that there is not always evidence that health events such as seizures are the direct result of caffeine toxicity.

Energy drink enthusiasts point out that the drinks often contain beneficial ingredients such as gingko biloba, which may improve memory, and açai berries, which are an antioxidant. Some who are opposed to bans and regulation describe the targeting of energy drink companies as reminiscent of political anti-tobacco campaigns that used children's health as an excuse to punish successful companies. They state that the health risks of tobacco are widespread and costly, while energy drinks provide a benefit in addition to the risks. Opponents of regulation also argue that in a free market system consumers should be able to make their own individual health and food choices.

1. The article presents arguments by those who propose barring energy drinks from the market and those who are opposed to a ban. In your response, analyze both positions to determine which one is best supported. Use specific evidence from the passage to support your claim.

Write your answer below or type your response on a computer. Take up to 45 minutes to respond.

The Writing Process

Draft

To provide details, paraphrase information from the passages. Explain the author's meaning and the connection to your ideas.

Use the questions on page 99 to evaluate your response.

2. A medical report says that, while 100 milligrams of caffeine might have some health consequences, it is generally safe for teenagers to consume 100 milligrams of caffeine in one day. Your city proposes two potential laws: a ban on drinks that contain more than 100 milligrams of caffeine per serving and a ban on selling energy drinks to anyone 18 or younger. Write a response in support of one of these laws over the other. Use specific evidence from the passage to support your claim.

Write your answer below or type your response on a computer. Take up to 45 minutes to respond.

> *Remember the Concept*
>
> Use a **Statement & Support** organizational structure for extended responses.
>
> Identify a central idea, supporting ideas, and conclusion. Find support for each of your ideas.

Use the questions on page 99 to evaluate your response.

Developing Ideas, Arguments, and Evidence

Good writing depends on good content. A developed idea or argument is one that you have thought about and looked at from various perspectives. You can describe your ideas in detail and make connections with other ideas.

The writing process helps you develop your ideas, arguments, and evidence so that you will have something compelling to say.

 Plan

When you begin to plan, you will identify ideas for your writing. What is your central idea? What are supporting ideas? During planning, find specific evidence and details to help develop your ideas.

 Draft

As you draft, you flesh out your ideas. Explain the connections between supporting ideas and your central idea, and explain the connections between details and your ideas. Defining connections is an important part of developing ideas.

 Evaluate

Evaluate whether your ideas are well developed. Do you give details and specifics?

This section will help you develop support for your ideas.

- **Developing Ideas**
  A developed idea is backed by details and explanations. Your idea is clearly communicated to the reader. This lesson will give you a strategy to develop your ideas.

- **Developing Strong Support**
  One of the most important types of writing is persuasive writing. In persuasive writing, you will state your position and present evidence to support that position. In this lesson, you will learn to evaluate the evidence that you use to support your ideas. The best support is specific, timely, accurate, and relevant.

- **Evaluating Arguments**
  Throughout life, you will read or listen to other people's arguments. Perhaps you will need to evaluate a scientific paper's conclusions. Perhaps you will need to make a decision about a ballot initiative or a candidate for governor. Perhaps you will need to write a report comparing applicants for a position at your company. In all of these circumstances, you will need to evaluate arguments. In this lesson, you will learn to evaluate and write about others' arguments.

- **Citing Evidence and Connecting with Claims**
  When you develop an argument, it is essential to make a connection between your evidence and your claim. This lesson gives you a strategy to build a "chain of evidence" connecting to your claim.

Developing Ideas

Have you ever . . .

- Given someone directions for a recipe?

- Run out of things to say when writing a paper?

- Read an email that didn't give you enough details?

The details are important. If you're explaining how to make a recipe, readers need enough information to make the recipe on their own. If someone sends you an email, you don't want that person to leave out important information. If you're writing a paper, you need enough details to fully explain your ideas. That's what **developing** your ideas means—giving enough information and explanation so that others can completely understand your meaning.

A developed idea is one that you have thought out fully. You have looked at it from different perspectives and described it in detail. A developed idea should have:

- Supporting ideas that give further information about your central meaning.

- Specific details that explain and support your idea.

- Explanations that connect supporting ideas, details, and the central idea.

The writing process helps you develop your ideas. When you plan, you think through your ideas. How are your ideas related? What details support your ideas? How do those details support your ideas? When you draft, you should continue to develop your ideas. Add explanations that make your ideas clear and show how your ideas and details are connected. As you work, you will evaluate your writing. Have you included all the details and explained all your thoughts?

Expand Your Ideas

Your ideas have more depth than you realize at first. Thinking through related ideas and supporting details helps you develop and communicate your ideas.

Imagine that you need to recommend one of your company's insurance policies to a coworker who anticipates having about $1,000 in medical expenses in the next year. The Bronze policy costs $55 per paycheck ($1,430 per year). It includes 20% coinsurance for most types of expenses, meaning that the insured person pays 20% of the expenses. Before any expenses are covered, you must pay a $1,500 deductible. The Silver policy costs $98 per paycheck ($2,548 per year). It includes 10% coinsurance for most types of medical expenses and has a $400 deductible. Your coworker wants to understand what her expenses will probably be like and what would happen if she had an unexpected large medical expense. Write an email explaining your recommendation.

Plan Ideas and Details

When you plan, expand your central idea, like blowing up a balloon. Add supporting ideas and details. What ideas are related to your central idea? What details help explain your ideas?

 1. Add your central idea, supporting ideas, and details to the graphic organizer.

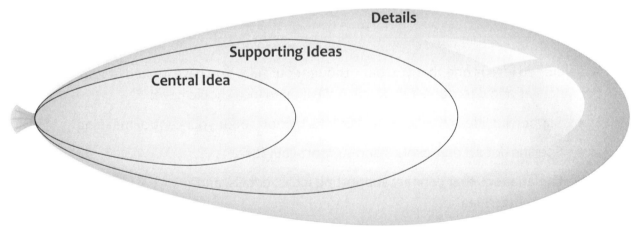

Your central idea might be to recommend the Bronze policy. One supporting idea is that the total expected expenses will be less. Another supporting idea is that unexpected expenses will not be too large a burden. Your details might include:

- The Bronze policy costs about $1,000 less per year.

- With the Silver policy, expected additional expenses are about $500. With the Bronze policy, expected additional expenses are about $1,000.

- The total savings with the Bronze policy is about $500.

- For an unexpected expense, the Bronze policy coinsurance would be 10% more of the expenses. The difference in the cost per paycheck approximately covers the difference in deductibles.

 ## Draft Ideas and Details

When you draft, expand your idea further by adding connections, explanations, and organization. Organize your thoughts in a logical order, and connect your ideas and details. Explain each idea and detail to develop your central idea.

? **2.** Draft a one paragraph response based on the graphic organizer.

You might write:

> I recommend the Bronze policy for your situation. Your total expected expenses for the year would be lower. The Bronze policy costs about $1,000 less per year out of your paycheck, and you would likely pay around $1,000 per year in medical expenses. The total costs would be about $2,500. With the Silver policy, your total costs would be about $500 more, because you would be paying $2,500 out of your paychecks plus a $400 deductible and 10% coinsurance on additional expenses. Large unexpected expenses would cost more, but the additional expenses wouldn't be too large a burden. The difference in the cost per paycheck approximately covers the difference in deductibles, so your main additional expense would be the coinsurance, which is 10% higher. If you are concerned about a potential large medical expense, you should consider the Silver policy. However, because of your low expected expenses, the Bronze policy is probably the better option.

 ## Evaluate Ideas and Details

Evaluate your work. Are there clear connections between your ideas? Do you fully explain your ideas and details?

? **3.** Evaluate, edit, and revise your response.

Submit

When you are satisfied with your response, check it one last time and then submit it. In this scenario, you would send the email.

Build Your Writing Skills

Write a response that recommends the other plan. Why might your coworker choose each plan?

Practice It!

Use the following passage for exercises 1 through 3.

Funding for NASA has come under fire as unnecessary government spending. Critics point to poverty, crime, unemployment, education, and other immediate issues that could benefit from the money spent on NASA, which had a budget of almost $18 billion in 2012. Those opposed to the space agency point to private space exploration projects such as SpaceX and Virgin Galactic as a better way to explore space in the future. The risks and costs of space exploration are great, critics say, while the benefits are intangible.

On the other hand, NASA supporters point out that the agency's budget is only 0.6% of the $3 trillion budget. The benefits may not be immediately tangible, but supporters say that those benefits are far-reaching. They point to the moon landing as an iconic moment in U.S. history that promotes science and technology. The money spent on space exploration has resulted in a long list of sometimes unexpected innovations "from solar panels to implantable heart monitors, from cancer therapy to light-weight materials, and from water-purification systems to improved computing systems" according to NASA[1].

[1] Source: "Benefits Stemming from Space Exploration" by the International Space Exploration Coordination Group, Sept. 2013, available at: http://www.nasa.gov/sites/default/files/files/Benefits-Stemming-from-Space-Exploration-2013-TAGGED.pdf

1. Write a response explaining which argument in the passage is stronger. Plan your response by using the following graphic organizer.

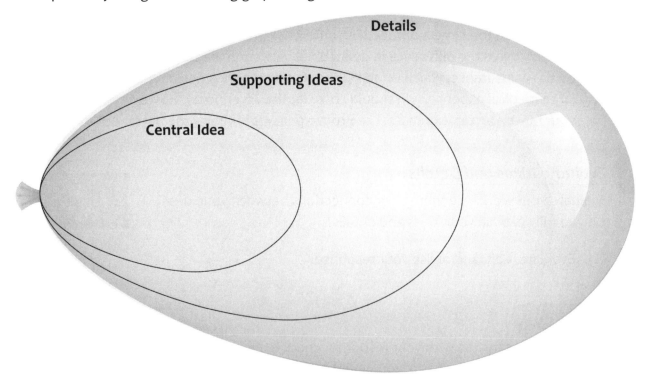

2. Draft your response. Organize your thoughts in a logical order, and connect your ideas and details. Explain each idea and detail to develop your central idea.

 3. Evaluate your response. Revise and edit your work until you are satisfied with your response.

Use the following passage for exercises 4 and 5.

Humans become infected with roundworms by drinking unfiltered water containing copepods (small crustaceans) which are infected with larvae of D. medinensis. Following ingestion, the copepods die and release the larvae, which penetrate the host stomach and intestinal wall. After maturation into adults and copulation, the male worms die and the females (length: 70 to 120 cm) migrate in the subcutaneous tissues towards the skin surface. Approximately one year after infection, the female worm induces a blister on the skin, generally on the distal lower extremity (foot). The blister ruptures, and when this lesion comes into contact with water, the female worm emerges and releases larvae. The larvae can then be ingested by a copepod. After two weeks, ingested larvae have developed into infective larvae. Ingestion of the copepods closes the cycle.

Source: Adapted from "Parasites—Dracunculiasis (also known as Guinea Worm Disease)—Biology" by the CDC. http://www.cdc.gov/parasites/guineaworm/biology.html

4. Parasites depend on hosts and live in or on the host's body. Explain how the parasite D. medinensis (roundworm) depends on hosts throughout its life cycle. Include multiple pieces of evidence from the passage to support your answer.

Plan your response by adding your central idea, supporting ideas, and details to the graphic organizer.

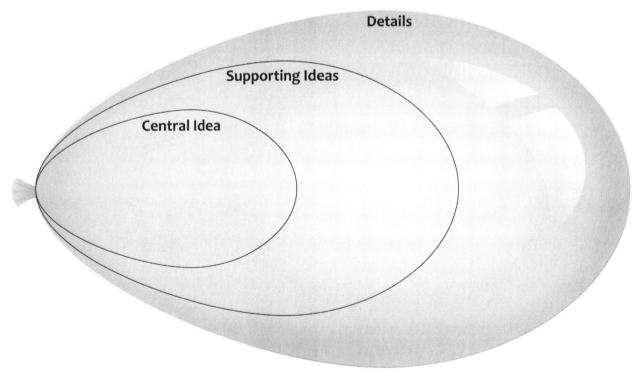

Details

Supporting Ideas

Central Idea

5. Draft and evaluate your response. Type your response on a computer if possible. If a computer is unavailable, use a separate sheet of paper.

Check Your Skills

Use the following passage for exercises 1 and 2.

The question of whether or not to raise the minimum wage periodically arises for states and for the federal government. Some workers are asking for a national minimum wage increase to $15 per hour, while many object that a higher minimum wage will stifle business and ultimately hurt the economy.

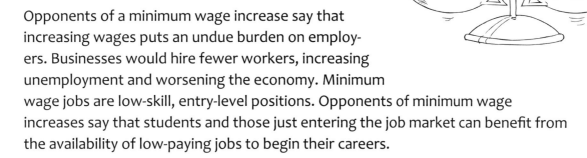

Opponents of a minimum wage increase say that increasing wages puts an undue burden on employers. Businesses would hire fewer workers, increasing unemployment and worsening the economy. Minimum wage jobs are low-skill, entry-level positions. Opponents of minimum wage increases say that students and those just entering the job market can benefit from the availability of low-paying jobs to begin their careers.

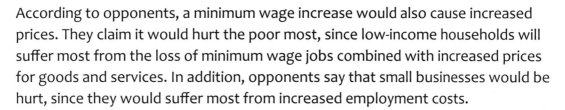

According to opponents, a minimum wage increase would also cause increased prices. They claim it would hurt the poor most, since low-income households will suffer most from the loss of minimum wage jobs combined with increased prices for goods and services. In addition, opponents say that small businesses would be hurt, since they would suffer most from increased employment costs.

An increased minimum wage puts money directly in the pockets of spenders, supporters state. Those working a minimum wage job spend money on food, transportation, and other necessities. An increase of minimum wage income would mean more money in the economy, spurring growth. A study by the Federal Reserve Bank of Chicago found that after the minimum wage was increased, households with at least one minimum-wage worker spent $700 more every three months. At the same time, an increased minimum wage would get many workers off of government assistance such as food stamps and welfare, supporters say.

Supporters of increasing the minimum wage note that the minimum wage has not kept up with inflation. In 2014, a full-time worker earning the federal minimum wage would make $15,080 a year. A family of four supported by two full-time minimum wage workers would be below the poverty level. Supporters of an increase state that a full-time job should pay a living wage, one that can cover basic living expenses.

1. The passage presents arguments supporting and opposing increasing the minimum wage. In your response, analyze both positions to determine which is best supported. Use relevant and specific evidence from the passages to support your response.

   Take approximately 45 minutes for this task. Use the space below for planning, and type your answer on a computer to prepare for computer responses. If a computer is unavailable, write your answer on a separate sheet of paper.

2. "A nation that continues year after year to spend more money on military defense than on programs of social uplift is approaching spiritual death. America, the richest and most powerful nation in the world, can well lead the way in this revolution of values.... There is nothing but a lack of social vision to prevent us from paying an adequate wage to every American citizen." —*Martin Luther King, Jr.*

   From *Where Do We Go from Here: Chaos or Community?* by Martin Luther King, Jr., 1967

   Develop an argument about how the passage reflects the issue expressed in the quotation. Incorporate relevant, specific evidence from the quotation, the passage, and your own knowledge of the contexts of the passages to support your analysis.

   Take approximately 25 minutes for this task. Use the space below for planning, and type your answer on a computer to prepare for computer responses. If a computer is unavailable, write your answer on a separate sheet of paper.

Remember the Concept

Expand your central idea by adding:

- Supporting ideas
- Details
- Connections
- Explanations

Use the questions on page 99 to evaluate your response.

Developing Strong Support

Have you ever...

- Changed a friend's mind?

- Almost agreed with someone's argument, until you learned the source of his or her information?

- Heard a rumor that you knew wasn't true?

Before people will agree with a claim, they will usually look for a reason to do so. "Because I said so," rarely works to persuade. To convince others to agree with a position, you must include strong support to back up your claim. Developing good support is crucial to creating a successful argument.

An argument includes a claim (the central idea that you want to prove), evidence, and reasoning. Evidence and reasoning is the support for your claim. With strong evidence and clear, logical reasoning, a claim can be convincing and persuasive.

Good evidence has four attributes. It is **Specific, Timely, Accurate,** and **Relevant.**

Each of these attributes helps create convincing support. Without all four of these attributes, a claim loses credibility, and the argument is not persuasive.

When evaluating your own support or analyzing others' arguments, test evidence by asking, "Is it **STAR Support**?"

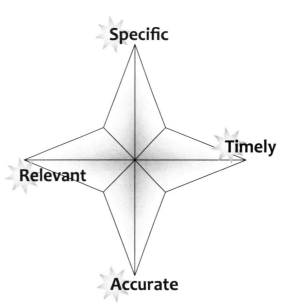

STAR Support

Specific, timely, accurate, and relevant evidence makes a claim more convincing.

- Look for STAR Support when you read and evaluate arguments.

- Use STAR Support in your own writing.

Ecotourism brings visitors to natural destinations to raise money and awareness to preserve natural environments. However, ecotourism is fundamentally flawed. It grows by 10 to 15 percent worldwide each year. That means more construction, trash, and use of local resources. An article in *USA Today* states, "one study in a Costa Rican national park found that wild monkeys turned into garbage feeders, becoming familiar with the presence of ecotourists and eating the food and rubbish left behind."[1] Ecotourism causes more harm than good. It is probably often developed in unsustainable ways, despite its stated goals.

[1]Source: From "Positive & Negative Effects of Ecotourism" by Rita Kennedy, Demand Media. *USA Today*, http://traveltips.usatoday.com/positive-negative-effects-ecotourism-63682.html

Evaluate What You Read for STAR Support

Are There Specific Facts?  **Specific**

To analyze an argument, find specific facts that the writer uses. If the writer uses no specific facts to support the argument, then the argument is mostly opinion.

? **1.** What specific facts does the writer use to support the argument?

The writer gives two specific facts: that ecotourism grows 10 to 15 percent each year and that a study showed wild monkeys began feeding on ecotourists' trash. The writer also makes two statements that are vague and unspecific: that ecotourism means more construction, trash, and use of resources and that ecotourism is developed in unsustainable ways.

Are the Facts Timely? **Timely**

The world is constantly changing, and new information is learned every day. Is the information used timely? If the writer is talking about the Great Depression, expect facts from the 1930s. If the writer is talking about the current drop-out rates, the facts should be recent.

? **2.** Is the evidence presented in the passage timely?

The passage doesn't give enough information to determine if the facts are timely without additional research. The facts may or may not be current.

Are the Facts Accurate?   ✦ Accurate

If an argument contains inaccurate facts, then the support is invalid. Misreadings, information used out of context, and second-hand knowledge can all lead to support that sounds great but is inaccurate. To spot inaccuracies, ask:

- Is the source credible?

- Does the information make sense?

?   **3.** Is the support for the argument accurate?

You can't always tell if information is accurate without checking other sources. However, you can tell that the author gives no sources for most of the facts. The only source is an article in *USA Today* that quotes an unnamed study. This source is a newspaper, which lends it credence, but the study itself would be a better source. The information in the passage makes sense, but the sources are vague.

Are the Facts Relevant?   ✦ Relevant

Do the facts actually support the claim? Examine the logical connection that the author makes between the fact and the central idea. Does it make sense?

?   **4.** Is the support for the argument relevant?

The statement that ecotourism involves construction, trash, and use of resources gives a reason that growth of 10 to 15 percent is relevant. Causing wildlife to eat garbage is a negative impact of ecotourism, though the author doesn't specifically state why it is a problem. The quotation is specific. However, facts about overall ecological impact of ecotourism (use of resources, impact of construction, and creation of trash) would be more relevant. The author's statement that ecotourism is developed in unsustainable ways is relevant, but it lacks any specific factual support.

The Writing Process

💡 **Plan**

Do not be mislead when you plan your writing. Irrelevant or inaccurate support is sometimes used to distract a reader from an argument.

Use STAR Support in Your Writing

When you write:

- Use **Specific** facts, incuding details, to support your argument.

- Use **Timely** facts when you are researching. Look at when an article or book was written.

- Use **Accurate** facts and check quotations. Do not misrepresent the author.

- Use **Relevant** facts. Explain how your facts support your claim.

5. Write a paragraph evaluating the strength of the author's argument. Use specific facts from the passage and include logical connections that show how the facts are relevant to your central idea.

You might write:

> The author's argument is not well supported. The author states that ecotourism grows 10 to 15 percent annually, but the passage lacks clear reasons why this growth is negative. It is logical that ecotourism results in construction, trash, and resource use, but what is the impact of construction? How much trash is generated? How many resources are used? How does this compare to the benefits of ecotourism? The author quotes one study that found wild monkeys in Costa Rica began eating trash from ecotourism. This is not a beneficial result. However, there are unanswered questions. How prevalent is this result in areas where there is ecotourism? Are there other studies with similar findings? The author states that ecotourism is "probably often developed in unsustainable ways," but gives no evidence for this statement. The use of the words "probably often" shows that the author is merely speculating. Ecotourism may be harmful, but the author does not make a convincing case.

Specific evidence includes an indirect quote ("ecotourism grows 10 to 15 percent annually") and a direct quote (" 'probably often developed in unsustainable ways' "). The indirect and direct quotes are accurate, and the response includes explanations of why the quotations show that the argument is not well supported. You can use direct quotes in your writing, but do not use too many. Restate ideas to show that you understand them.

The Writing Process

Plan

Verify facts before you use them in an argument.

Developing Strong Support

Use the following prompt to complete exercises 1 through 3.

Imagine your city council is hearing arguments for and against reopening an abandoned drive-in movie theater. The developer is requesting some taxpayer money to contribute to the renovation and in return pledges to have a free family movie night every other month for the first two years.

 1. Which of the following is irrelevant to the developer's argument?

    a. The movie theater would increase business in an otherwise unsightly area.

    b. The theater would draw visitors from out of town and support other businesses.

    c. The movie theater used to show a double feature every Saturday night.

    d. People who remember the theater support its renovation.

 2. Which specific information would help the developer make his case stronger?

    a. How renovating drive-in theaters has spurred economic growth in similar towns

    b. Why the theater closed down

    c. What movies would show there over the next three years

    d. Information about the current movie theatre that shows movies indoors

 3. A local citizen argues: "It is unfair for taxpayers to pay for business development. A drive-in theater would just encourage young people to drink in their cars. When the theater was open in the 1980s, it caused a lot of traffic. This theater is a bad idea."

    a. Does the argument provide specific facts? How does this affect the argument?

    b. Does the argument provide timely facts? How does this affect the argument?

    c. Does the argument provide accurate facts? How does this affect the argument?

    d. Does the argument provide relevant facts? How does this affect the argument?

Use the following passage for exercises 4 and 5.

Our city should install sidewalks along all our paved streets. Currently, only 50% of our streets have sidewalks beside them. This puts our children and all pedestrians in danger as they walk to school, stores, and neighbors' homes. Our citizens should not be afraid to walk to the park or the grocery store. Last year, two people were injured because they were hit by cars as they walked along the shoulder of a street. One is paralyzed and confined to a wheelchair. The benefits of installing sidewalks surely outweigh the cost. We require bicyclists to wear helmets; we should have roads with sidewalks. It is a matter of our safety.

---

 4. Examine the passage for STAR Support.

   a. What is the best example of specific evidence in the passage? Why?

   b. What one sentence is an example of irrelevant support? Why?

   c. What statement in the passage has questionable accuracy? Why?

5. Using STAR support, write a paragraph evaluating the argument in the passage.

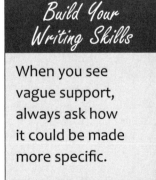

Build Your Writing Skills

When you see vague support, always ask how it could be made more specific.

Check Your Skills

Use the following passages for exercise 1.

National Parks Are Best Preserved by Government

Despite the claim that privatizing the National Park system would create a stronger and more accessible collection of travel destinations, the best protector of national parks is national government. As a non-profit institution, the function of government is to preserve democracy—and therefore the symbols of democracy—for citizens. Once public lands leave public control, they may be lost forever. Preservation is far from certain once a private corporation controls the land.

In the past, private industry has attempted to purchase state parks. In most cases, this has resulted in less public access at a greater cost to each visitor. The government created the parks; the government should keep control of them. The government may not be a perfect steward. However, for the people's land, the people's government is still the most appropriate regulator.

Privatizing Can Better Preserve and Maintain

National Parks should be turned over to private corporations to run. As seen in other resources once regulated as monopolies, such as telephone services and some utilities, private corporations can manage large projects more efficiently, sometimes so efficiently that profit is possible. The 20th century has seen truly hideous mismanagement of national forests and parks, with amenities and roads in disrepair, parks understaffed, and safety of campers and hikers left to suffer. The 21st would only see the continuation of shutdowns and poorly staffed parks. Our treasured wilderness areas and monuments deserve better.

The United States has long stood as an example of how private industry can revolutionize industries. National parks should be seen as tourist destinations as well as national legacies. Private industry has outperformed government in creating destinations of choice and should be permitted to apply its models of efficiency to the national park system to ensure that our treasures remain standing and accessible through the 21st century.

1. Analyze the two arguments to determine which position is best supported. Use relevant and specific evidence from both pssages to support your response.

   Write your answer below or type your response on a computer. Take approximately 45 minutes to respond.

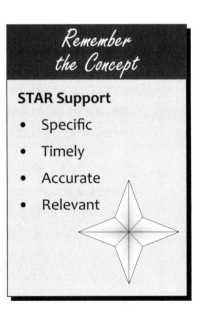

Remember the Concept

STAR Support

- Specific
- Timely
- Accurate
- Relevant

Use the questions on page 99 to evaluate your response.

Evaluating Arguments

Arguments can be crafted to make you respond emotionally or to seem logical, even if they are not. Many arguments sound perfectly reasonable the first time you read or hear them. On further examination, you may begin to see weaknesses.

A successful argument proves its claim using relevant evidence and sound reasoning. To evaluate whether an argument is credible and sound, describe the elements of the argument:

- Is its claim clear?

- Is the evidence credible?

- Is the speaker reliable?

After you describe the claim, evidence, and speaker, use this information to write an evaluation of the argument.

Speaker

Claim

Evidence

MATERIAL EVIDENCE

Describe the Claim, Evidence, and Speaker

When you evaluate an argument, you aren't giving your own opinion of the topic. Your goal is to objectively analyze the author's argument. This skill will help you write about arguments and make decisions about controversial topics.

When you describe the claim, evidence, and speaker, you assign value. For example, if you describe a claim as unreasonable and unclear, then it is not a strong claim. If you describe evidence as specific, credible, and from a trusted source, it is strong evidence.

Examine the following argument.

Two years of college education should be available free to all qualified U.S. students. By 2018, over 60 percent of jobs will require workers with at least some college education, but public support of education is down in 48 states. At the same time, employers are cutting back (or at least not expanding) their training programs. They are, in essence, expecting candidates to show up fully qualified, according to an article in the *Las Vegas Review-Journal*.[1]

Two years of free postsecondary education would address the problem of filling jobs with qualified workers. Government investment in free higher education would stimulate the economy by allowing college graduates more spending capacity. More people would attend college if finances weren't a barrier. Other countries who make this investment see a payoff in the quality of their work forces and lifestyles.

The benefits of this policy are obvious. Students would be more motivated to graduate high school, knowing that they have options after they graduate. Under this policy, students would decide immediately on a major or training program best suited to them and would be more likely to finish quickly and begin working.

Currently, a college degree is out of reach to many students, limiting their potential. A lack of college education prevents young adults from being financially stable enough to support a family, buy a home, or start a business. Even those who graduate college aren't assured of financial security. Those who leave college owing thousands in student loans and still can't find work are in grave financial situations. A free two-year degree would help many young people get started in careers. This would benefit individuals and also the society to which they contribute.

[1] "By 2018, 60 percent of job openings will require college education," Eli Amdur, *Las Vegas Review-Journal*, available at http://www.reviewjournal.com/news/education/2018-60-percent-job-openings-will-require-college-education

Describe the Claim

First, identify the claim. The claim is the idea that the writer is attempting to prove. Summarize the claim in one sentence. Then, describe the claim. You can use the following words to describe the claim and identify your reasoning.

Claim

Negative ➡	Claim	⬅ Positive
Unreasonable	Somewhat reasonable	Reasonable
Unclear	Somewhat clear	Clear

? 1. Identify and describe the claim of the argument, giving reasons for your description.

The claim is clear: that two years of college education should be free to U.S. students. It is stated at the beginning of the argument. The claim is somewhat reasonable. The government provides many services and could expand public education by two years. However, this would incur significant costs and changes in the educational system.

Describe the Evidence

Evidence

Use **STAR Support** criteria to examine the evidence. Is it **Specific**, **Timely**, **Accurate**, and **Relevant**? Be sure to evaluate the source. Is the source untrustworthy or unknown? Is the source an expert?

Evidence must also be **sufficient**. There must be enough evidence to prove the claim. Use the following words to describe evidence.

Negative ➡	Evidence	⬅ Positive
Insufficient/vague	Some evidence	Specific
Out-of-date	Unknown date	Timely
Inaccurate	Unknown source	Accurate
Irrelevant	Somewhat relevant	Relevant

? 2. Describe the evidence in the argument, giving reasons for your description.

One piece of evidence that is specific, timely, accurate, and relevant is that over 60% of jobs will require degrees by 2018. This fact comes from a newspaper article. Other statements are vague, such as the idea that students would quickly decide on majors. This idea isn't supported by specifics and seems mainly to be speculation. It has no source. Overall, the evidence seems insufficient, especially since it does not address the costs of the proposal.

Speaker

Describe the Speaker

The speaker is the author of an argument. Some speakers are biased, such as a company trying to sell a product. Others are reliable experts.

Many speakers are unknown, except through their arguments. A speaker who makes contradictory statements or uses emotional pleas to distract from the argument is not trustworthy. Also examine how the speaker addresses arguments from the opposition. Does the author ignore opponents?

Negative ➡	Speaker	⬅ Positive
Untrustworthy/biased	Unknown	Expert
Ignores or misrepresents	Acknowledges opponents	Addresses legitimate
opponents		counterarguments

?   **3.** Describe the speaker, giving reasons for your description.

The speaker's expertise or bias is unknown. He or she acknowledges that the opposition exists but does not address any counterarguments. The speaker is also somewhat contradictory. The statement that college graduates often cannot find jobs undermines the idea that two years of free college is a solution.

Write an Evaluation

Combine your descriptions of the claim, speaker, and evidence to write an evaluation. Start with a central idea that states the overall strength or weakness of the argument and use specific details to explain your descriptions of the claim, speaker, and evidence. Your evaluation should have a beginning, middle, and ending.

?   **4.** Write a paragraph evaluating the argument.

See the Answers and Explanations section on page 113 for a sample response.

Practice It!

Holiday parades are a waste of public resources. They are admittedly festive and happy occasions, but they serve no civic purpose that couldn't be otherwise served by a concert, fireworks show, or fair. Marching bands can be heard at football games, and balloons and floats are simply unnecessary diversions.

At famous parades, such as the Macy's Thanksgiving Day Parade or Mardi Gras, viewers, who are often inebriated, gather in the streets only to watch other people walk at various speeds. These parades block traffic and create trash. They require police and emergency responder overtime. This cost would be better spent funding environmental programs, shelters, education, and other public services.

 1. Describe the claim in the passage, giving reasons for your description.

 2. Describe the evidence in the passage, giving reasons for your description.

 3. Describe the speaker in the passage, giving reasons for your description.

 4. Write a well-organized paragraph evaluating the argument. Include suggestions to improve the argument.

The Writing Process

⚙️ **Evaluate**

When you evaluate your writing, describe your claim, evidence, and yourself as a speaker. Look for ways to develop your reliability as a speaker. One way is by acknowledging the opposition and respectfully responding to counterarguments.

Use the following passage for exercises 5 through 8.

Driverless cars are our future, and we should encourage their development by passing laws allowing driverless cars on roads throughout the country. Nevada, Florida, and California already have laws allowing driverless cars. These software-controlled cars have successfully navigated San Francisco's steep and twisting Lombard Street and driven over 300,000 miles of tests. Only one accident has happened during testing: a human driver rear-ended a driverless car. With their incredible record of safety, driverless cars will reduce drunk driving, make commutes more productive, and reduce insurance costs. In a March 2012 video posted by Google, a legally blind man goes through a drive-through in a self-driving Toyota Prius. This video highlights the benefits of driverless car technology to disabled people. Why not allow this safe and beneficial technology to flourish?

 5. Describe the claim in the passage, giving reasons for your description.

 6. Describe the evidence in the passage, giving reasons for your description.

 7. Describe the speaker in the passage, giving reasons for your description.

 8. Write a well-organized paragraph evaluating the argument. Include suggestions to improve the argument.

> **Build Your Writing Skills**
>
> To compare two arguments, compare your evaluations of the claim, evidence, and speaker. It will help you determine which argument is stronger and why.

Check Your Skills

Use the following passages for exercise 1.

The presence of royalty gives a nation a sense of pride and history that should be cherished and honored. Great Britain is an excellent example of what a royal family can add to the culture. The constitutional monarchy allows Britain to experience the best of both worlds: the continuity of tradition and the progressive possibilities of a democracy.

Around the world, people celebrate royal weddings and births. When Prince Charles and Lady Diana married, it was an international sensation. An estimated 750 million people watched. The birth of Prince George of Cambridge in 2013 spurred composer Paul Mealor to write a new lullaby, "Sleep On." Shared events like this bring a nation together, forming cultural milestones.

In Great Britain and other nations with historic monarchies, the royal family is a link to the past. Although royal roles may be ceremonial, a royal family allows the average citizen to celebrate a shared history and national pride.

The family of the Prince of Wales: Engraving by Shyubler. Published in the magazine *Niva*, published by A.F. Marx, St. Petersburg, Russia, 1888

Royalty devalues the average citizen. A monarchy flies in the face of the idea that "all men are created equal." If royalty were eliminated, any loss of tradition would be more than replaced by a thirst for innovation, improvement, and individuality.

Through its monarchy, Great Britain makes a silent statement that some people are inherently better than others. Members of the royal family have special treatment because of an accident of birth. In an article on CNN, Graham Smith details the problems with British monarchy: "It is secretive, having recently lobbied successfully to have itself removed entirely from the reaches of our Freedom of Information laws; it lobbies government ministers for improvements to its financial benefits and for its own private agenda; it is hugely costly—an estimated £202 million a year."[1] The British monarchy is outdated, undemocratic, and costly. On the other hand, the U.S. system of democracy, where anyone might earn the presidency, encourages self-improvement because birth is not destiny.

[1]Source: "Why UK should abolish its 'failed' monarchy" by Graham Smith on CNN.com
http://www.cnn.com/2012/05/30/world/europe/uk-jubilee-republicans/index.html

1. Analyze the two arguments to determine which position is best supported. Use relevant and specific evidence from both passages to support your response.

   Write your answer below or type your response on a computer. Take approximately 45 minutes to respond.

Remember the Concept

Describe the **claim**, **evidence**, and **speaker** to evaluate an argument.

Use the questions on page 99 to evaluate your response.

Citing Evidence and Connecting with Claims

Connections

Have you ever...

- Realized halfway through a movie how it would end and told your reasons to a friend?

- Explained how you found the solution to a problem?

- Gave evidence for your opinion in an argument?

Evidence is important. When you make a decision, you use evidence to come to a conclusion. When you speculate about what will happen, you use evidence to form an opinion. When you solve a problem, you use evidence to find a solution.

When you make a claim—an idea you want to prove—you will need to back up that claim with evidence. Imagine that you want to show that a character in a story is selfish. Your evidence is that the character takes a prize away from his best friend. You need to show why taking the prize was selfish. It is important that you make a clear connection between your claim and the evidence that you present. The reader needs to understand *why* the evidence supports the claim. When you connect evidence with your claim, you show the reader your reasoning and make your argument more convincing.

Your writing needs a strong chain of reasoning.

- You need strong evidence that supports your writing.

- You need a strong connection between the evidence and your claim.

- You need a strong claim that is supported by the evidence.

If all the links of the chain are in place, your writing will present a convincing argument.

Building a Chain of Evidence

Build a chain of evidence by defining the claim and evidence, making connections, and organizing your argument in a logical way.

Imagine that you need to recommend a candidate to interview for a sales position. The following are summaries of two candidates' resumes. Examine the summaries and write a paragraph recommending one of the two candidates.

Miguel Velasquez has a BS in English and went to school on a scholarship. He has two years of sales experience. He says that he is looking for a position where he can grow with the company and that he enjoys helping customers find the products they need.

Angela Goren has a BA in communications and a year and a half of sales experience. She says that she has used your products and enjoys them. She also says she can clearly communicate the benefits of your products to customers. In her last sales job, she received a promotion after six months.

Identify the Claim

The claim is your point of view. Your chain of evidence proves your claim, so the claim is the foundation of the argument. The claim should be clear and specific.

?   **1.** Identify the claim for your recommendation.

Your claim might be that Angela Goren is the better candidate for the job because of her familiarity with the company and her success in sales. To decide on a candidate, ask: Which claim can I support with the evidence?

Define the Evidence

Strong evidence makes a strong chain. Because you have identified your claim, you should already have ideas about your evidence. Find specific details that support your claim.

?   **2.** Define two to four specific pieces of evidence from the passage to support your claim.

You might identify the following evidence for choosing Angela:

- She has a BA in communications.
- She is familiar with the company and its products.
- She received a promotion in her former job.

Explain the Connection

For each piece of evidence, write a sentence explaining the connection with the claim. Why does it support the claim?

? **3.** For each piece of evidence, write a sentence explaining why it supports your claim.

You might write:

- Because of her BA in communications, Angela may have good communication skills.
- Because she knows the company's products, Angela may need less training.
- Because she received a promotion after six months, Angela has shown skill in sales.

Organize the Evidence and Connections

Organize your chain of evidence. Begin with your claim, and then put your evidence in a logical order. Include your connections for each piece of evidence.

? **4.** Organize your claim, evidence, and connections.

You might decide to put the most convincing evidence first and start by talking about her promotion, then her familiarity with the company, and finally her BA in communications.

Draft, Evaluate, and Submit

Use your organized claim, evidence, and connections to finish drafting your work.

? **5.** Draft and evaluate your recommendation on a computer or a separate sheet of paper.

See the Answers and Explanations section on page 115 for a sample recommendation.

Use the following passage for exercises 1 through 3.

Today, Mars is cold and dry, and liquid water is not stable on the surface. However, more than 3.5 billion years ago, climatic conditions appear to have been favorable for the presence of liquid water. How did its climate produce conditions favorable for rainfall and runoff? Most effort has been focused on proposing that the early Martian atmosphere was different because of a different mass and composition.

Carbon dioxide, methane, and SO_2 get the most attention, but each has its own unique issues and problems. Clouds form in CO_2 atmospheres that may limit the greenhouse potential, and vast beds of carbonates have not yet been detected as would be expected when CO_2 and liquid water coexist for extended periods of time. Methane requires a large continuous source to counter its removal by photolysis. And SO_2 may not build up to high enough levels to be effective since it readily oxidizes to sulfate aerosols which can cool the surface.

Another possibility is that wet conditions on early Mars were created by large impact events, which induced significant climate change. It is obvious that impactors have pummeled the Martian surface in the distant past. These could have temporarily altered the climate and produced episodes of intense rainfall.

Source: Adapted from NASA AMES Mars Climate Modeling Group, "Early Mars." http://spacescience.arc.nasa.gov/mars-climate-modeling-group/past.html

1. Compare the possible reasons that the passage gives for warm, wet conditions on early Mars. Explain which reason seems most logical.

   a. Identify your claim.

   b. Define two to four pieces of evidence.

    c. For each piece of evidence, write one sentence connecting it to the claim.

    d. Organize your claim, evidence, and connections in a logical sequence.

2. Draft your response based on your claim, evidence, and connections.

3. Evaluate your response. Revise and edit your work until you are satisfied with your response.

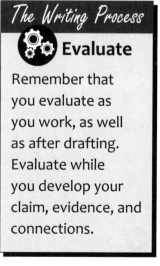

The Writing Process

Evaluate

Remember that you evaluate as you work, as well as after drafting. Evaluate while you develop your claim, evidence, and connections.

Use the following passage for exercises 4 and 5.

Many school districts are removing drink machines from schools or replacing them with machines dispensing bottled water. Supporters of removing the machines state that sugary drinks, including soda, sugared teas, and sports drinks, contribute to childhood obesity and add little nutritional value. Teenagers get about 15% of their calories from beverages, and a recent study found that where only sodas are banned from campuses, students still bought as many sugary drinks.

Some opponents, however, point to the study as evidence that drink bans are ineffective. The study found that in schools that banned all sugary drinks, students still consumed the same quantity of those drinks. The policies only lowered access to sugared drinks at school. Opponents recommend that schools focus on health education instead of eliminating free choice. They also point out that drink sales provide needed revenue for schools and protest that eliminating a source of school funding is unwise.

 4. Evaluate the arguments for and against drink machines in schools. Write a response supporting a claim that one position is best supported.

    a. Identify your claim and two to four pieces of evidence.

    b. For each piece of evidence, write one sentence connecting it to the claim.

    c. Organize your claim, evidence, and connections in a logical sequence.

 5. Draft and evaluate your response. Type your response on a computer if possible. If a computer is unavailable, use a separate sheet of paper.

Check Your Skills

Use the following passage for exercises 1 and 2.

Net neutrality is an important and often misunderstood political issue. The term *net neutrality* means ensuring that all websites have equal access to Internet bandwidth, so that individual websites such as Netflix or YouTube can't be slowed or blocked by Internet providers (ISPs) such as cable and phone companies. According to a recent court ruling, the FCC does not have the right to enforce net neutrality without declaring ISPs as common carriers, which are necessary utilities such as electricity or water.

Supporters of net neutrality are concerned that ISPs could charge websites for bandwidth, limiting online competition, development and innovation of new websites, and the availability of free web services. The prices of web-based services could rise if ISPs began charging websites for bandwidth.

Those in favor of net neutrality are also concerned that ISPs could ban or charge competitors, while starting their own competing web services. Some suggest that ISPs could ban any website or service for any reason, including political reasons. Companies could theoretically block news services, organizations, or blogs that they oppose, or they could stop consumers from posting content on Twitter or Facebook, perhaps even banning any posts that criticize the ISPs.

Opponents of net neutrality want an open market for ISPs. An unregulated Internet, they state, means the ability to experiment with new business practices and innovate ways to improve the Internet. Those who want deregulation are concerned that net neutrality means increasing government power over business. They are in favor of businesses competing in a free market, without regulation. They argue that classifying Internet providers as utilities is stifling to business.

Without net neutrality, opponents say that ISPs will be able to manage Internet bandwidth better. Large-scale Internet services, such as websites that stream high-resolution videos, use a large portion of bandwidth. With net neutrality, the costs for this high usage by large companies are pushed onto consumers, opponents say.

1. The passage presents arguments supporting and opposing net neutrality. In your response, analyze both positions to determine which is best supported. Use relevant and specific evidence from the passages to support your response.

   Take approximately 45 minutes for this task. Use the space below for planning, and type your answer on a computer to prepare for computer responses. If a computer is unavailable, write your answer on a separate sheet of paper.

2. "A wise and frugal government, which shall restrain men from injuring one another, shall leave them otherwise free to regulate their own pursuits of industry and improvement, and shall not take from the mouth of labor the bread it has earned—this is the sum of good government." —*Thomas Jefferson*

   From the First Inaugural Address by Thomas Jefferson, 1801

   Develop an argument about how the passage about net neutrality reflects the issue expressed in the quotation. Incorporate relevant, specific evidence from the quotation, the passage, and your own knowledge of the contexts of the passages to support your analysis.

   Take approximately 25 minutes for this task. Use the space below for planning, and type your answer on a computer to prepare for computer responses. If a computer is unavailable, write your answer on a separate sheet of paper.

> *Remember the Concept*
>
> **Build a Chain of Evidence**
>
> - Identify the Claim
> - Define the Evidence
> - Explain the Connections
> - Organize the Evidence

Use the questions on page 99 to evaluate your response.

Writing Practice

The best way to improve your writing is by practicing. When you write, you are communicating your ideas to your readers. If you can clearly and effectively communicate, you will be more successful in the workplace, in school, and in every-day tasks.

To improve, focus on using the writing process as you practice.

Plan: Don't start writing until you have planned. Read, think, and define what you want to write.

Draft: Drafting will be easier if you have planned well. Organize what you want to say, and add connections, explanations, and transitions.

Evaluate: Think critically about your writing. Check that you have a clear, logical organization, specific details, and effective language. Revise and edit your writing to improve it and eliminate errors.

Submit When you are satisfied with your writing, do one last check for errors. Do any final formatting, and submit your work. That might mean hitting "send" on a email or turning in a paper to your instructor.

As you work, be sure to self-evaluate your performance. To self-evaluate your practice, use the questions on page 99.

This section includes:

- **Practice for Reasoning through Language Arts**
  Learn a process to evaluate and compare opposing arguments about a variety of topics. This type of writing will improve your analytical skills and allow you to communicate your critiques of written materials.

- **Practice in Social Studies Writing**
  Social studies writing involves analyzing works from many time periods. The same issues affect people in different eras and cultures. Learn to make connections between past and present ideas.

Practice for Reasoning through Language Arts

Have you ever...

- Made a choice between two products?

- Explained to someone why you made a decision?

- Tried to convince a friend how to vote in an election?

If you have, then you have compared two arguments, evaluated them, and drawn conclusions. Evaluating conflicting points of view is a valuable skill. You might need to evaluate candidates for a job, companies who provide a service, or competing products. In college courses, you might evaluate competing hypotheses or interpretations of topics in sociology, economics, or literature.

Reasoning through Language Arts means using reading and writing to think and reason. When you reason using language arts, you evaluate what you read and express your evaluation in writing. Often, this involves evaluating and comparing logical arguments.

To evaluate and compare arguments, identify the opposing claims and the support for each claim. Which argument has the stronger support? What are the strengths and weaknesses of each argument?

Evaluating and comparing arguments is not about your personal opinion. It is about the strength of the arguments. You might disagree with strong arguments or agree with weak ones. Your goal is to objectively evaluate the strength of arguments, whether or not you agree with them.

Comparing Arguments with the Writing Process

The following prompt asks you to compare two arguments. You need to evaluate the arguments and then build your own argument about the information in the passage.

The passage presents arguments both supporting and opposing a 10 cent tax on grocery bags. In your response, analyze both positions to determine which one is best supported. Use relevant and specific evidence from the passage to support your response. Take approximately 45 minutes for this task.

On Thursday, the city council heard speakers on the proposal to require grocery stores to charge a 10 cent tax per bag for disposable grocery bags. The following is a summary of arguments from supporters and opponents.

Speakers supporting the proposal stated that a tax on bags would reduce waste by encouraging shoppers to bring their own bags. They cited the wide availability of inexpensive reusable bags and noted that grocery stores use a high volume of both paper and plastic bags, producing significant waste.

Plastic grocery bags cannot be recycled in the city's curbside recycling program and have a low rate of recycling, according to information provided by the city's recycling contractor and local supermarkets. The tax revenue would be used to improve the city's recycling and green energy programs. Those improvements could include distributing free reusable bags to some consumers.

Speakers opposing the proposal stated that a 10 cent tax would be a burden on consumers. They stated that stores should have a choice whether or not to provide bags to consumers and that consumers should have a choice whether to invest in reusable bags. The proposal effectively forces consumers to either pay a tax or buy reusable bags.

Speakers stated that since groceries are not taxed to avoid undue burdens on the impoverished, grocery bags should not be taxed either. One speaker called the proposal a "forgetful consumer tax," noting that shoppers who forgot their bags at home would be charged. Opponents also stated that grocery bags are likely to be reused by consumers, who will have to buy more garbage bags and other products to use at home.

Plan: Build the Framework (15 minutes)

Start by planning your response. Compare writing your response to constructing a building. You need a framework before you can complete the walls and roof.

- Central Idea: Which argument in the passage is stronger? Explain your reasoning.
- Details: Identify details that support your idea, and explain the connection.
- Conclusion: Summarize and expand on your central idea. Explain your conclusion.

1. Plan your response to the prompt.

Central Idea:	Explanation:
Restate a Detail:	Explanation:
Restate a Detail:	Explanation:
Restate a Detail:	Explanation:
Restate a Detail:	Explanation:
Conclusion:	Explanation:

You might write:

Central Idea: Proponents have a stronger argument.	Explanation: Their argument includes more specific data than the opposition.
Restate a Detail: Supporters say plastic grocery bags are inconvenient to recycle and are recycled less often than other items.	Explanation: This data is from a reliable source and shows the waste produced by the current system.

Restate a Detail: Opponents say a 10 cent tax is a burden.	Explanation: This statement doesn't include any data to support it, but could be a strong argument with supporting data.
Restate a Detail: Opponents point out groceries have no tax because food is a necessity. They compare the grocery bag tax to this.	Explanation: The statement sounds logical, but the impact on poorer consumers is still not established.
Restate a Detail: Opponents say consumers will reuse grocery bags and buy other bags if grocery bags are taxed.	Explanation: This is speculation.
Conclusion: The opposition's argument lacks data.	Explanation: The opposing argument could be stronger, but it needs data to show the burden on the consumer.

Draft: Construct the Structure (20 minutes)

Use your central idea, details, and conclusion to construct your response. Your introduction should include your central idea and explanation. Use the details you identified to write the body, and end with the your conclusion.

?   4. Draft your response.

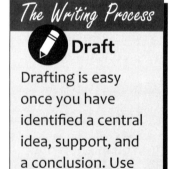

The Writing Process

Draft

Drafting is easy once you have identified a central idea, support, and a conclusion. Use your planning as the framework when you draft your response. Add transitions and more explanation.

You might write:

> Based on the passage, the proponents of charging the tax on grocery bags have a stronger argument. Their argument includes more specific data than the opposition, which lacks good support for its ideas.
>
> The supporting argument is based on the idea that reducing waste should be a societal goal. The argument identifies grocery bags as a problem. Supporters say plastic grocery bags are inconvenient to recycle and are recycled less often than other items. This data is from a reliable source. Given this information, reducing the use of disposable grocery bags seems a reasonable goal.
>
> The opposition fails to clearly support its claims. Opponents say a 10 cent tax is a burden but do not include any data to support this statement. How much of a burden would the tax create? Supporters suggest that tax revenues might finance a free reusable bag program, but the opposition doesn't respond to this. However, the potential burden on consumers could be a strong argument if it included data about the impact on consumers.
>
> Opponents point out groceries have no tax because food is a necessity. They compare the grocery bag tax to this policy. This is a logical argument based on existing tax laws, but the impact on poorer consumers is still not established. Other items sold at grocery stores are taxed, including toilet paper and soap, and grocery bags are not food items.
>
> One of the more problematic claims of the opposition is that consumers will reuse grocery bags and buy other bags if grocery bags are taxed. This is speculation. The author cites no source and gives no specific data. The use of the word "likely" shows that the argument is speculative instead of based on facts.
>
> The opposition's central idea is that taxes are a burden and that consumers should be left to choose the best path. The supporters' argument is based on the value of eliminating waste and the wastefulness of grocery bags. The opposition's points are arguably more weighty; this tax might unfairly affect the poor. However, those arguing against the tax need data to show the burden on the consumer.

 ## *Evaluate and Submit: Add Finishing Touches (10 minutes)*

In a timed response, be sure that you evaluate your work as you write. Organize your response around a strong central idea and include specific details. Explain the significance of quotations from the passage. Take a few minutes after you draft to review, revise, and edit your work. Improve your writing and eliminate errors. When you are satisfied with your response, submit your work.

Practice It!

The passages present arguments both supporting and opposing increased oil drilling in the Gulf of Mexico. In your response, analyze both positions to determine which one is best supported. Use relevant and specific evidence from the passages to support your response. Take approximately 45 minutes for this task.

The U.S. has natural reserves of oil in the Gulf of Mexico that are not being utilized, although they could improve our economy, lower consumer costs, and increase government revenues.

Domestic oil production means more jobs to boost local economies. Oil is a massive industry that should be encouraged to promote our economy. While creating jobs, an increased oil supply will also mean lower gas prices. Local oil reserves also eliminate the need to transport oil across the ocean and reduce our dependence on foreign oil.

In addition to these benefits, state and federal governments will see increased revenue from leases to oil companies for drilling. Some are concerned about safety and the environment. However, with modern technology, oil can be drilled safely, without harming wildlife and natural environments. There is no reason to let oil reserves sit at the bottom of the Gulf of Mexico, unused.

Further drilling in the Gulf of Mexico is unnecessary and dangerous. Our money would be better spent elsewhere. Deep-water oil drilling is an extreme risk to the environment and likely to produce more harm than benefits. Oil spills are common occurrences. They disrupt local industries, including fishing and tourism, while oil companies do little to correct the damages. Saying that it won't happen again is naive. The Deepwater Horizon spill in 2010 spilled almost five million barrels of oil. Oil cleanup continued for a year, and damage to human health, fishing and tourism, and marine habitats continue today. The damage to the environment and wildlife is also costly.

In addition to the hazards, oil drilling only increases the damage fossil fuels cost to our environment. There are only 18 billion gallons of off-shore oil reserves in the entire U.S. coastline, extending our oil reserves perhaps two and a half years. Spending money investing in clean energy such as wind and solar would be more productive than investing in costly, damaging oil production.

1. Complete the graphic organizer to plan your response. Take approximately 15 minutes to plan your response.

Central Idea:	Explanation:
Restate a Detail:	Explanation:
Restate a Detail:	Explanation:
Restate a Detail:	Explanation:
Restate a Detail:	Explanation:
Conclusion:	Explanation:

 2. Draft a response to the prompt based on the graphic organizer. Take approximately 20 minutes to draft your response based on your planning. Type your answer on a computer to prepare for computer responses. If a computer is unavailable, write your answer on a separate sheet of paper.

3. Evaluate, revise, and edit your response. Make sure your ideas are organized and connected logically and check for errors. Take approximately 10 minutes for this task.

Use the following passages for exercises 4 through *6.*

The passage presents arguments both supporting and opposing buying pets from breeders. In your response, analyze both positions to determine which one is best supported. Use relevant and specific evidence from the passages to support your response. Take approximately 45 minutes for this task.

Pet breeders are a popular way to buy a particular pet suited to a particular taste. However, pet breeders come under fire because shelters are filled with unwanted dogs and cats. The controversy over pet breeders is not likely to end soon.

Pet breeders and buyers of purebred pets often accuse opponents of unfairly lumping respectable breeders in with breeders who mistreat dogs. They say that, while abuses should be punished, breeders fill an important function.

A prospective pet owner, supporters state, has a right to choose a pet that is appropriate to his or her lifestyle. According to the U.S. Humane Society, almost 40% of dogs are returned to a breeder, given to a shelter, euthanized or abandoned within a year. A lack of compatibility is a primary reason that pets are abandoned, according to supporters of breeding. Dogs and cats that are adopted from shelters often have physical or emotional problems that will cause problems for pet owners, proponents of breeders state. Breeders help match prospective pet owners with suitable pets.

On the other hand, those opposed to breeders cite health problems found in many purebred dogs. Inbreeding causes a high risk of cancer, heart disease, arthritis, skin diseases, and neurological disorders. Bulldogs have breathing difficulties because of their purebred features; basset hounds suffer from spinal, skin, and joint issues. Golden retrievers are particularly susceptible to cancer.

Opponents also state that dog breeding encourages and legitimizes puppy mills and backyard breeders that mistreat dogs and keep them in unhealthy conditions to make an easy dollar off the high demand for purebred dogs. With thousands of rescued dogs and cats in shelters, opponents of breeders maintain that prospective pet owners can be matched with appropriate pets without breeding.

4. Complete the graphic organizer to plan your response. Take approximately 15 minutes to plan your response.

Central Idea:	Explanation:
Restate a Detail:	Explanation:
Restate a Detail:	Explanation:
Restate a Detail:	Explanation:
Restate a Detail:	Explanation:
Conclusion:	Explanation:

5. Draft a response to the prompt based on the graphic organizer. Take approximately 20 minutes to draft your response based on your planning. Type your answer on a computer to prepare for computer responses. If a computer is unavailable, write your answer on a separate sheet of paper.

6. Evaluate, revise, and edit your response. Make sure your ideas are organized and connected logically and check for errors. Take approximately 10 minutes for this task.

Check Your Skills

Use the following passages for exercise 1.

Nuclear power is a necessary part of a clean energy plan to help reduce our dependence on fossil fuels and limit the effects of global climate change. Nuclear power plants do not release carbon dioxide or other pollutants into our atmosphere; they only emit steam. Nuclear energy is the most important source of clean energy available today, producing cheaper energy than wind power, solar power, or coal.

Accidents have happened at nuclear power plants, including the recent disaster at Fukushima, but these incidents are preventable with good oversight, planning, and regulation. The Fukushima power plant began operation in 1971, and newer plants are safer and more reliable. We should not let fear keep us from clean, inexpensive energy that we can produce with today's technology.

Nuclear power is unsafe and a poor investment for our future. In 2011, the Fukushima nuclear plant was hit by a tsunami, and hundreds of thousands of residents were put in danger of radiation exposure and increased cancer risks. This incident shows the dangers of nuclear power to humans and the environment. Massive amounts of radiation were released, and it will take years to clean up the affected water.

Accidents aren't the only danger from nuclear power. Hazardous waste remains radioactive for thousands of years, stored in concrete basins. There is no solution for eliminating this waste except storing it indefinitely. While solar power is fast becoming cheaper and more efficient, nuclear power remains expensive. Cost estimates that suggest nuclear is cheaper leave out expenses such as construction and waste storage. With advancing technology, we have better options than nuclear.

1. The passages present arguments both supporting and opposing nuclear power. In your response, analyze both positions to determine which one is best supported. Use relevant and specific evidence from the passages to support your response.

Take approximately 45 minutes for this task. Type your answer on a computer to prepare for computer responses. If a computer is unavailable, write your answer on a separate sheet of paper.

Use the questions on page 99 to evaluate your response.

Use the following passage for exercise 2.

In the United States, only nine states do not have laws banning text messaging for all drivers. Text message bans are meant to keep drivers from distractions and prevent accidents. However, some people object to the laws as ineffective and unnecessary.

Opponents to cell phone bans note that there are already laws against driver distractions. They recall laws that lowered speed limits to 55 miles per hour to pre-vent accidents. Drivers still sped; in fact, speeding was the norm on many highways. Anti-texting laws will be the same, opponents say. In fact, texting will be more dangerous, because drivers will try to hide their mobile devices, creating more distractions. As evidence, oppo-nents cite a study of insurance claims in four states covering several months before and after a texting-while-driving ban. The study shows that accidents increased by nine percent.

Others dismiss this study, calling for more long-term studies that do not only focus on the first few months of a new regulation. Proponents of laws against texting while driving cite statistical evidence that texting is hazardous while driving. The FCC states that 11% of 18- to 20-year-old drivers who survived car accidents reported that they were sending or receiving texts at the time of the crash. In a survey by the Pew Research Group, 40% of American teens reported being in a car when the driver put people in danger by using a cell phone. A single text message takes the driver's eyes off the road for approximately 4.6 seconds, according to the U.S. Department of Transportation. During that time, a car driving 55 miles per hour will travel the length of a football field.

 2. The passage presents arguments both supporting and opposing bans on texting while driving. In your response, analyze both positions to determine which one is best supported. Use relevant and specific evidence from the passages to support your response.

Take approximately 45 minutes for this task. Type your answer on a computer to prepare for computer responses. If a computer is unavailable, write your answer on a separate sheet of paper.

Use the questions on page 99 to evaluate your response.

Use the following passage for exercise 3.

Since New York City's 2013 attempt to limit soda sizes in restaurants to 16 ounces or less, the availability of large soda sizes has become a topic of controversy. Many people objected to the limit as excessive government regulation. Others supported it as an initiative to improve public health.

The goal of the ban on large soda sizes was to limit consumption of sugared drinks with little or no nutritional value. Those supporting the ban cite the public health costs of obesity. In 2010, the U.S. Centers for Disease Control (CDC) reported 35.7% obesity among American adults. The estimated health costs related to obesity, including indirect costs, are over $100 billion. Supporters state that large sized sodas are unnecessary and only contribute to obesity. According to the Center for Science in the Public Interest, sugared drinks are the largest source of calories for Americans, accounting for approximately seven percent of calories per day.

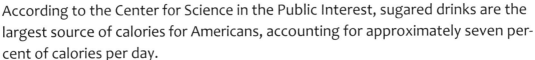

Those who oppose a ban on large drinks claim that it is an unnecessary regulation that limits business, interferes with consumers' free choice, and does not attack the root problems of obesity. Some argue that targeting one type of food is unjustified, when no one food causes obesity. Others note that there are no studies on the effectiveness of banning large sugared sodas. Sugared sodas are known to cause weight gain, but the results of regulations and limits on soda sizes are unknown. Since nearly 80% of sugared sodas are sold in stores that wouldn't be affected by a restaurant ban, the regulation would probably not affect the regular soda drinkers who would most benefit from a reduction in sugar intake.

 3. The passage presents arguments both supporting and opposing limits on soda sizes in restaurants. In your response, analyze both positions to determine which one is best supported. Use relevant and specific evidence from the passages to support your response.

Take approximately 45 minutes for this task. Type your answer on a computer to prepare for computer responses. If a computer is unavailable, write your answer on a separate sheet of paper.

> *Remember the Concept*
>
> **Plan:** Build the Framework
>
> **Draft:** Construct the Structure
>
> **Evaluate:** Add the Finishing Touches
>
> **Submit**

Use the questions on page 99 to evaluate your response.

Practice in Social Studies Writing

Have you ever...

- Used the phrase "all men are created equal"?

- Argued with a friend about whether a new law was constitutional?

- Voted for a presidential candidate?

The U.S. government is built on fundamental principles outlined in the Constitution and other founding documents. The country's founders considered principles such as freedom, equality, representative government, privacy, and justice. Throughout U.S. history, we have debated and changed our ideas about these fundamental and lasting concepts.

Events throughout U.S. history—the Civil War, the American Civil Rights Movement, prohibition, the Great Depression, the internment of Japanese-Americans during World War II—have affected our views of governance. The discussion is not over. Is freedom more important than security? What do we mean by an equal society? What are just punishments? Concepts such as liberty and self-determination have spurred dialogue, change, and even war. The U.S. Constitution addresses these concepts, yet there is still active and passionate discussion about many of these issues today.

Enduring social issues are important to us all. They shape our culture and our laws. This lesson will give you practice thinking and writing about fundamental issues in society and the links between the past and the present.

The Relationship Bridge

The following prompt asks you to do an important task: identify and explain the relationship between two expressions of an enduring issue at different times or places. In your response, you will build a bridge between the two passages.

Develop an argument about how President Bush's speech reflects the enduring issue expressed in the quotation from Nelson Mandela. Incorporate relevant and specific evidence from the quotation, the passage, and your own knowledge of the historic contexts of the passages to support your analysis. Take approximately 25 minutes for this task.

For to be free is not merely to cast off one's chains, but to live in a way that respects and enhances the freedom of others.

—*Nelson Mandela*

Source: From *Long Walk to Freedom* by Nelson Mandela, 1995

Three weeks ago we celebrated our nation's Independence Day. Today we're here to rejoice in and celebrate another "independence day," one that is long overdue. With today's signing of the landmark Americans with Disabilities Act, every man, woman, and child with a disability can now pass through once-closed doors into a bright new era of equality, independence, and freedom....

This historic act is the world's first comprehensive declaration of equality for people with disabilities—the first. Its passage has made the United States the international leader on this human rights issue.... Our success with this act proves that we are keeping faith with the spirit of our courageous forefathers who wrote in the Declaration of Independence: "We hold these truths to be self-evident, that all men are created equal, that they are endowed by their Creator with certain unalienable rights." These words have been our guide for more than two centuries as we've labored to form our more perfect union. But tragically, for too many Americans, the blessings of liberty have been limited or even denied. The Civil Rights Act of '64 took a bold step towards righting that wrong. But the stark fact remained that people with disabilities were still victims of segregation and discrimination, and this was intolerable. Today's legislation brings us closer to that day when no Americans will ever again be deprived of their basic guarantee of life, liberty, and the pursuit of happiness.

—*President George H.W. Bush, July 26, 1990*

Source: From "Remarks of President George Bush at the Signing of the Americans with Disabilities Act," July 26, 1990, available at http://www.eeoc.gov/eeoc/history/35th/videos/ada_signing_text.html

Plan: Describe the First Passage (2 minutes)

To build a bridge, you first need to build bridge ends. Examine one passage first. This will help you quickly organize your thoughts, especially in a timed exercise.

- Read the prompt and the first passage.
- Identify the societal issue in the passage and what you know about the context.
- Summarize the opinion.

? 1. Identify the issue in the quotation from Nelson Mandela and summarize the opinion.

Bridge End	Connection	Bridge End
Issue: Summary: Context:		Issue: Summary: Context:

The issue in this quotation is freedom. The opinion is that we should not only be concerned with our own freedom, but with others' freedoms. The clue to the context is its author, Nelson Mandela, who fought against the racial segregation of Apartheid in South Africa.

Plan: Describe the Second Passage (4 minutes)

Repeat the process with the second passage. In this case, the second passage is longer. As you read, write down the quotations from the passage that describe the speaker's perspective well. This will help you build evidence to use in your writing.

? 2. Identify the issue in the second passage and summarize the opinion.

Bridge End	Connection	Bridge End
Issue: Freedom Summary: We should be concerned with others' freedoms, not just our own. Context: Apartheid		Issue: Summary: Context:

The context of the passage is the Americans with Disabilities Act. Bush says the ADA enhances freedom by removing discrimination against people with disabilities. You might choose some key quotes: "a bright new era of equality, independence, and freedom;" "first comprehensive declaration of equality for people with disabilities;" "But the stark fact remained that people with disabilities were still victims of segregation and discrimination."

Plan: Your Thesis (4 minutes)

Fill in the connection between the two passages by defining the relationship between the two perspectives. State the relationship in a full sentence that you can use as a thesis.

? 3. Write your thesis, joining the ideas in the two passages.

Bridge End	Connection	Bridge End
Issue: Freedom Summary: We should be concerned with others' freedoms, not just our own. Context: Apartheid		Issue: Freedom Summary: The ADA enhances freedom by removing discrimination against disabled people. Context: ADA

Your thesis might be: "The Americans with Disabilities Act (ADA), which enhances freedom by removing discrimination against people with disabilities, fulfills Nelson Mandela's vision of finding freedom in ensuring others' freedom."

Draft (10 minutes)

Once you have written your thesis, you are ready to draft. Use your bridge as a reference as you write, incorporating your ideas about each passage to support your thesis. Start with your thesis to write your introduction. Use evidence from each piece of writing in the body. Then end your draft with a clear conclusion.

? 4. Draft your response.

You might write:

> The Americans with Disabilities Act (ADA), which enhances freedom by removing discrimination against people with disabilities, fulfills Nelson Mandela's vision of finding freedom in ensuring others' freedom. President Bush speaks about ending the "segregation and discrimination" affecting those with disabilities. Mandela's experience was with segregation and discrimination based on race. Both emphasize the need to protect freedom for all in a just society.
>
> President Bush calls the ADA an entrance into "a bright new era of equality for people with disabilities." The means to this equality is ensuring access to education, service, and jobs. The ADA mandates making public services accessible to those with disabilities. This is a mandate for the government to "respect and enhance" the freedom of Americans with disabilities. It levels the playing field so that individuals are not held back by their disabilities, but have the same opportunities as others.
>
> As the "first comprehensive declaration of equality for people with disabilities," the ADA was groundbreaking in providing new freedoms. Similarly, Nelson Mandela broke new ground in South Africa, where black citizens were once limited in where they could live and what they could do. While black South Africans were restricted by unfair laws, Americans with disabilities have historically been restricted by a lack of accessible services. Without a wheelchair ramp, a courthouse or school is inaccessible to someone without use of their legs. In South Africa, unfair laws were removed; the ADA removed barriers by building wheelchair ramps and other adaptations for those with disabilities. Both actions created more individual freedom and opportunity.
>
> Bush clearly connects those with disabilities to other groups who have experienced discrimination: "But the stark fact remained that people with disabilities were still victims of segregation and discrimination." He evokes the same idea of freedom in the quote by Nelson Mandela. Freedom hinges on expanding freedom for all by removing barriers and creating opportunity.

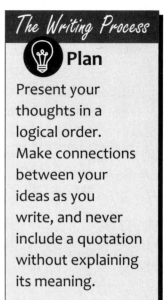

The Writing Process

Plan

Present your thoughts in a logical order. Make connections between your ideas as you write, and never include a quotation without explaining its meaning.

Evaluate and Submit (5 minutes)

In a timed response, be sure that you evaluate your work as you write. Organize your response around a strong central idea, and include specific details. Explain the significance of quotations from the passage. Take a few minutes after you draft to review, revise, and edit your work. When you are satisfied with your response, submit your work.

Practice It!

Use the following passages for exercises 1 and 2.

Develop an argument about how the letter to the editor reflects the enduring issue expressed in the quotation from Benjamin Franklin. Incorporate relevant and specific evidence from the quotation, the passage, and your own knowledge of the contexts of the passages to support your analysis. Take approximately 25 minutes for this task.

They who would give up essential Liberty, to purchase a little temporary Safety, deserve neither Liberty nor Safety.

—*Benjamin Franklin*

Source: From the Pennsylvania Assembly's Reply to the Governor, Nov. 11, 1755, by Benjamin Franklin

---

The U.S. government is taxed with assuring our security, but it is also taxed with securing our liberty. Without personal liberty, security is a burden instead of a boon. The actions of the NSA in collecting information about massive numbers of U.S. citizens with only the oversight of secret courts robs us of our liberty and disrupts the difficult balance of liberty and security.

One of the foundations of intelligence services is secrecy, so individual liberty is often compromised. The important question is, when does individual privacy and liberty outweigh security concerns? Targeting suspected individuals, based on known evidence, is one thing. Collecting massive amounts of data from U.S. citizens indiscriminately invites abuses.

How are we to know that this data won't be abused for personal or political reasons? Should we not fear the potential corruption of our government? Data is a powerful tool. Massive, secret data collection is a frightening tool.

I know that many people fear terrorist attacks in the United States. Fear, though, has never been the basis of good governance. Good governance requires the rational weighing of important goals. It requires establishing a balance of values. We value security and protection. We also value liberty and freedom from unjust prosecution. The massive collection of phone and Internet data does not retain a balance between these values.

—*Lara Conroy, Letter to the Editor*

1. Complete the graphic organizer to summarize each passage and write a thesis.

Bridge End	Connection	Bridge End
Issue:		Issue:
Summary:		Summary:
Context:		Context:

 2. Draft and evaluate a response to the prompt based on the bridge graphic organizer. Use a computer or draft your response in the workbook.

Use the following passages for exercises 3 and 4.

Develop an argument about how the blog post reflects the enduring issue expressed in the quotation from Carl Schurz. Incorporate relevant and specific evidence from the quotation, the passage, and your own knowledge of the contexts of the passages to support your analysis. Take approximately 25 minutes for this task.

The Senator from Wisconsin cannot frighten me by exclaiming, "My country, right or wrong." In one sense I say so too. My country; and my country is the great American Republic. My country, right or wrong; if right, to be kept right; and if wrong, to be set right.

—*Carl Schurz*

Source: From remarks in the U.S. Senate, February 29, 1872, by Carl Schurz

---

I have heard many stories of citizens being harassed for taking cell phone videos of police officers. Recently, only blocks from my apartment, a police officer reportedly took a cell phone from a pedestrian who was filming an arrest. Events like this are worrying to me. Police officers have authority and power; they should be scrutinized.

On the other hand, some communities are experimenting with filming all police officers on duty by making officers wear body cameras as part of their uniforms. The University of South Florida Department of Criminology and the Orlando Police Department are currently studying the effects of body cameras. Personally, I believe this study will show their value. In discussion groups, police officers I've talked to have applauded the use of body cameras. They believe that cameras integrated into police uniforms will stop many people from false complaints and help police officers avoid violent confrontations. That is one side of the story. If police officers are abusing their powers, cameras should also stop the harassment of undeserving citizens.

None of us wants to be filmed constantly or have our privacy compromised by surveillance. However, filming of on-duty police officers is a different matter. Police officers are public servants performing a public duty. They must be subject to oversight in their work.

—*Antonio Marquez, Blog Post*

3. Complete the graphic organizer to summarize each passage and write a thesis.

Bridge End	Connection	Bridge End
Issue: Summary: Context:		Issue: Summary: Context:

 4. Draft and evaluate a response to the prompt based on the bridge graphic organizer. Use a computer or draft your response in the workbook.

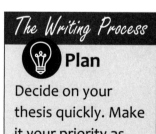

The Writing Process

Plan

Decide on your thesis quickly. Make it your priority as you read. Look for specific evidence as you define your thesis.

Check Your Skills

Use the following passages for exercise 1.

. . . nor shall any person be subject for the same offense to be twice put in jeopardy of life or limb; nor shall be compelled in any criminal case to be a witness against himself, nor be deprived of life, liberty, or property, without due process of law; nor shall private property be taken for public use, without just compensation.

—*Fifth Amendment to the U.S. Constitution*

Source: Bill of Rights, available at http://www.archives.gov/exhibits/charters/bill_of_rights_transcript.html

---

In June 2013, the U.S. Supreme Court ruled that silence could be used to prosecute suspects in a court of law. In the case of Salinas v. Texas, the suspect did not answer whether he thought his shotgun would match the shells from the murder scene. The prosecution used his silence as evidence against him. Suspects in criminal cases must be read their Miranda rights so that they understand their constitutional rights, including the right to remain silent. The Supreme Court ruled that because the defendant "did not expressly invoke" the Fifth Amendment right to remain silent, this right was then void.

In other words, the right to remain silent is only in effect if you state that you are taking advantage of that right (not merely if you remain silent). It seems to me that the idea of an inherent right is that you do not have to invoke the right. The right is inalienable—a right that cannot be removed. This Supreme Court ruling takes away the right to remain silent by requiring magic words to activate it. Isn't the right to remain silent simply the right not to speak? If you remain silent, you are invoking that right, whether or not you state it explicitly to the police.

—*Vera Morgan, Letter to the Editor*

---

 1. Develop an argument about how the letter to the editor reflects the enduring issue expressed in the quotation from the U.S. Constitution. Incorporate relevant and specific evidence from the quotation, the passage, and your own knowledge of the contexts of the passages to support your analysis.

Take approximately 25 minutes for this task. Type your answer on a computer to prepare for computer responses. If a computer is unavailable, write your answer on a separate sheet of paper.

Use the questions on page 99 to evaluate your response.

Use the following passages for exercise 2.

The one pervading evil of democracy is the tyranny of the majority, or rather of that party, not always the majority, that succeeds, by force or fraud, in carrying elections.

—*Baron John Emerich Edward Acton*

Source: Baron John Emerich Edward Acton, *The History of Freedom and Other Essays*, 1907

One of the most significant problems facing our society today is fair and representative districting. Democracy only works if our votes are represented. However, in too many states, those in power have drawn boundary lines of districts in order to stay in power.

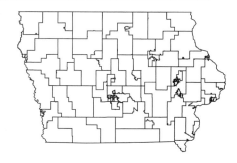

Someone must draw and approve boundary lines for districts, but any politician doing so faces a conflict of interest. The shape of a politician's district, and the demographics of the people in that district, can dictate whether he or she can win the next election.

The only way to avoid unfair districts is to take districting decisions out of the hands of politicians. In 2010, the state of California created a non-partisan redistricting commission composed of five Democrats, five Republicans, and four members not affiliated with either major party. The commission was given criteria for equitable districts with reasonable geographic boundaries without regard for benefits or costs for incumbent politicians. Redistricting can be difficult, but this non-partisan independent commission is a step in the right direction. All of our states need to follow the path of independent redistricting to assure every citizen representation in the government. I have come to believe that this is a national problem and should be dealt with on the national level. Too many states will not implement fair redistricting on their own.

—*Elijah Banner, Letter to Senator*

---

 2. Develop an argument about how the letter reflects the enduring issue expressed in the quotation from Baron Acton. Incorporate relevant and specific evidence from the quotation, the passage, and your own knowledge of the contexts of the passages to support your analysis.

Take approximately 25 minutes for this task. Type your answer on a computer to prepare for computer responses. If a computer is unavailable, write your answer on a separate sheet of paper.

Use the questions on page 99 to evaluate your response.

Use the following passages for exercise 3.

We are now forming a republican government. Real liberty is neither found in despotism or the extremes of democracy, but in moderate governments.

—*Alexander Hamilton*

Source: Alexander Hamilton, debates of the Federal Convention, June 26, 1787

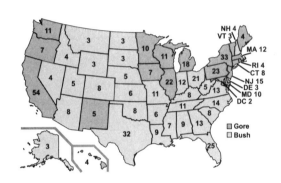

The electoral college is an outdated feature of our democracy. No one goes into a voting booth to vote for an electoral college representative. We vote for the presidential candidates. Shouldn't our votes count, one for one across the nation, in the election of our President?

The debate over the electoral college often focuses on the 2000 presidential election. Democratic candidate Al Gore won the popular vote by over 500,000 votes. However, because of the electoral college system, the election went to Republican candidate George W. Bush. Each state sends representatives to the electoral college based on the election outcome in that state. This makes it possible for a candidate to win the popular vote and lose the election. While some consider this result to be a fluke, it happened. It could happen again, by a larger margin. Our democracy should count each voice, not each state.

Isn't it more democratic to vote directly for presidential candidates? Why should our federal government depend on a state-by-state count of electoral college representatives? It's time to do away with the electoral college.

—*George Olsen, Blog Post*

 3. Develop an argument about how the blog post reflects the enduring issue expressed in the quotation from Alexander Hamilton. Incorporate relevant and specific evidence from the quotation, the passage, and your own knowledge of the contexts of the passages to support your analysis.

Take approximately 25 minutes for this task. Type your answer on a computer to prepare for computer responses. If a computer is unavailable, write your answer on a separate sheet of paper.

Remember the Concept

Create a Relationship Bridge to define the relationship between two passages.

Use the questions on page 99 to evaluate your response.

Self-Evaluation of Your Writing

Evaluating your writing is an important skill. Use the following questions to rate your writing and identify problems. The more you practice the writing process and evaluate your results, the more your writing will improve. When you use the following questions, try to identify specific examples from your writing that show your writing's strengths and weaknesses.

You may make copies of this section to evaluate multiple writing assignments. Not every question will apply to every task, so you may skip evaluation questions that are not appropriate to the assignment. Average the scores for each question to rate your response as (3) excellent, (2) acceptable, or (1) not acceptable.

When you receive feedback from an instructor, compare the feedback to your self-evaluation. This will help you learn to evaluate your writing more effectively.

Creation of Arguments and Use of Evidence

1. How well do you create original logical arguments and set up a central idea or purpose that is connected to the prompt?
   (3) Exceptionally Well: The purpose is focused and clearly connected to the prompt.
   (2) Somewhat/Sometimes Well: The argument may stray from the purpose at times but typically shows some connection to the prompt.
   (1) Not Well: An argument may be present but lacks purpose or does not connect to the prompt.

2. How well does your writing use relevant and specific evidence?

   (3) Exceptionally Well: Evidence and explanations are specific and directly support the purpose. Evidence is from a reliable source.

   (2) Somewhat/Sometimes Well: Evidence may be loosely related or not relevant at times. More evidence may be needed.

   (1) Not Well: Evidence is lacking or does not come from a reliable source.

3. How well does your response evaluate the arguments in the passage?

   (3) Exceptionally Well: The response thoroughly analyzes the arguments in a passage. This includes evaluating claims, identifying assumptions or logical fallacies, and determining the credibility of sources.

   (2) Somewhat/Sometimes Well: The response partially analyzes the arguments and issues in the source text. Analysis may be too basic, limited, or include inaccuracies.

   (1) Not Well: The response minimally analyzes the issue or the argument presented in the source text. The response may completely lack analysis or show no understanding of the argument.

4. How could you improve in this category?

Development of Ideas and Organizational Structure

1. How well does your writing logically develop ideas and elaborate your central ideas with relevant details?

   (3) Exceptionally Well: Ideas are well developed and easy to follow. Most ideas are explained and supported.

   (2) Somewhat/Sometimes Well: Some ideas are not fully developed or are vague.

   (1) Not Well: Some ideas are not sufficiently developed or do not completely make sense. There is little elaboration of central or supporting ideas.

2. How well does your writing create a progression of ideas from one to the other that ties details to your central idea?

   (3) Exceptionally Well: The ideas progress in a way that makes sense. There is a clear connection between the main points and details that further develop them.

   (2) Somewhat/Sometimes Well: The ideas progress but details may be disorganized or fail to connect to supporting ideas or the central idea.

   (1) Not Well: The ideas are undeveloped or fail to make sense. There is little to no elaboration of ideas.

3. Does your writing have a clear organizational structure that supports your purpose?

   (3) Exceptionally Well: The writing is organized in a way that shows the message and purpose. The writing uses effective transitions.

   (2) Somewhat/Sometimes Well: The organization of the writing is inconsistent or only partially effective. Transitions are used inconsistently.

   (1) Not Well: The writing has no clear organization and lacks effective transitions.

4. How well does your writing establish a style and tone that is appropriate to its intended audience and purpose?

   (3) Exceptionally Well: The writing uses a formal style and tone that shows awareness of the audience and purpose of the task.

   (2) Somewhat/Sometimes Well: The writing uses an inconsistent formal style and tone that shows awareness of audience or purpose.

   (1) Not Well: The writing uses an ineffective or inappropriate tone that demonstrates limited or no awareness of audience or purpose.

5. How well do you choose words and use a strong vocabulary?

   (3) Exceptionally Well: The writing includes specific, well-chosen words that help express ideas.

   (2) Somewhat/Sometimes Well: The writing may occasionally include misused words or words that vaguely express ideas.

   (1) Not Well: The writing includes frequent misused words, slang, or vague or repetitive language.

6. How could you improve in this category?

Clarity and Command of Standard English Conventions

1. How well does your writing apply the following: good spelling, correct subject-verb agreement, correct pronoun use, good use of modifiers and word order, correct capitalization, correct use of apostrophes, and correct use of punctuation?

   (3) Exceptionally Well: The writing correctly uses the above conventions.

   (2) Somewhat/Sometimes Well: There may be some misuse of the above conventions.

   (1) Not Well: There are many errors in the above conventions.

2. How well does your writing apply the following: correct clauses and parallel structure, good phrasing without awkwardness or wordiness, good transitions, correct sentence structures without run-ons and fragments, and good word usage?

   (3) Exceptionally Well: The writing shows correct use of sentence structure and flows together.

   (2) Somewhat/Sometimes Well: There may be some awkward sentences that make the meaning unclear. The writing flows well in places.

   (1) Not Well: Sentences are consistently awkward, choppy, repetitive, rambling, and meaning is unclear.

3. How well does your writing avoid errors in mechanics and conventions?

   (3) Exceptionally Well: There may be minor errors that do not interfere with understanding.

   (2) Somewhat/Sometimes Well: There may be many errors in mechanics and conventions that occasionally affect understanding.

   (1) Not Well: The writing does not demonstrate understanding of conventions and usage of language.

4. How could you improve in this category?

Answers and Explanations

This section provides answers and explanations for this workbook, including sample responses to prompts. There are many ways to approach writing tasks. The answers here give you examples of effective responses. Keep in mind that strong arguments can be made for either side of a debated issue. Some explanations include examples of ineffective responses, as well, which you can use to practice revision. Use these samples along with the self-evaluation questions in this workbook to help you evaluate and improve your writing.

The Writing Process page 3

Plan, Draft, Evaluate page 5

Plan, Draft, and Evaluate Your Writing

Practice It! *pages 8–10*

1. Since the topic is likely unfamiliar, the best way for Sharon to begin planning is to read and research. While reading, she can brainstorm, take and organize notes, ask questions, and focus on a specific central idea. Once she has preliminary planning done, she can brainstorm again and organize her ideas.

2. Writing about a topic that is too general often results in poor writing. Narrowing the focus to a specific central idea is an important part of planning, drafting, and evaluating. To decide on a central idea, Andrew can research Congress, look at news articles, and read about historical topics. Andrew can make notes about interesting ideas and do some preliminary research to make sure he has access to enough information about the potential topics. Then, he needs to decide which idea is most interesting and best suited to writing a paper.

3a. Before Ralph begins writing, he should think about the information he has about his department's productivity. Does he need to do additional research? What is the best way to organize the report? What information does he need to cover? What kind of introduction and conclusion does he need?

3b. Ralph can draft an outline of his report and determine what sections he needs to write. He can organize his notes into sections and then use the outline and notes to write his draft.

3c. Ralph can evaluate his writing by reviewing his draft and making sure it's organized well and makes sense. He might ask, does it give enough information? Is the information easy to understand? Are the conclusions well supported? Does Ralph make reasonable suggestions?

4a. Mauricio is in the planning stage of the writing process. He has found some books and has brainstormed information he knows. He still needs to complete the planning stage before writing.

4b. A good way for Mauricio to proceed would be to read and research more information about submarines. He will need to take notes, ask questions, think about the information, and determine his central idea. Once he has a clear, focused central idea, he can organize his notes to prepare for drafting.

5a. The purpose is to show that you can clearly explain possible advantages of predicting solar flares based on the passage. No audience is specified, so the audience is an instructor or reader who will evaluate your writing. You can identify the effects of solar flares from the passage. Predicting solar flares will help with predicting these effects.

5b. You might write:

Predicting solar flares can provide benefits for government and business. Since long-distance radio signals are affected by solar flares, forewarning could allow radio broadcasters to prepare for interruptions. Satellite orbits are also vulnerable to solar flares. Predicting their occurrence could help NASA and other space agencies to correct satellite orbits and minimize damage. Solar flare prediction would help both business and government to be prepared. Innovators might even find ways to make solar flares beneficial by utilizing their effects.

5c. Evaluate your paragraph's organization, central idea, supporting details, and conclusion. Make sure your paragraph is clear and easy to understand.

6. Revising your work as you evaluate it might involve reorganizing, adding details, rewriting sentences for clarity, or adding transitions. Depending on your task, you could completely rewrite your work. On the other hand, proofreading work when you are finalizing it is a smaller task. You might format your work, correct small spelling or grammar errors, or make minor changes to add clarity. The major revisions should be done when you draft and evaluate, before you are ready for final proofreading.

7a. The purpose is to critique an argument. Since no audience is specified, you will want to show your ability to evaluate and analyze the argument, showing both its good points and its problems. You might plan to identify the writer's specific arguments and evaluate their strengths and weaknesses.

7b. You might write:

The author's argument in favor of closing Bradley Branch Library is coherent but weak. The author argues that library services are being replaced by Internet services. While many resources are available over the Internet, libraries provide free access to books, magazines, and little-used research materials difficult to find elsewhere. Only limited books are available online without costs. Modern libraries also provide free access to the Internet, to assure that online resources are available across the community. The author "doubts" that the library is busy, showing that he or she is merely speculating. The author also says that patrons can travel to another branch, but the author does not acknowledge that residents with limited transportation who can benefit most from a local library might find traveling difficult. Overall, the author would benefit from additional research regarding the library's offerings and uses.

7c. Evaluate your paragraph's organization, central idea, supporting details, and conclusion. Make sure it is clear and easy to understand.

8. If you were writing a blog post about a recipe, you might plan your post by outlining the recipe, taking photos, making the recipe to test it, and brainstorming ideas for your introduction and conclusion. You could draft the post based on your planning and then evaluate it to make sure the recipe is clear and easy to follow. You also might want to evaluate whether your post is interesting for readers. Once your post is finalized, you can publish it to your blog.

Check Your Skills
pages 11–12

1. The following is an example of an **effective** response. It includes specific details, follows a logical order, and has an introduction and conclusion.

Lee is experiencing a common problem among writers. Instead of fully utilizing the writing process, he focuses primarily on drafting. The result is writing that lacks content and is not thoughtfully crafted. Lee should begin by planning his writing, instead of jumping into the drafting stage. In the planning stage, Lee can research information about building a shed, as well as drawing from his own knowledge to brainstorm ideas. He should identify a focused central idea to help him organize his writing and create a strong introduction. He can organize his prewriting into an outline to help him write his first draft. As he plans and drafts, Lee should evaluate his work for clarity and good organization. He should also evaluate his work after he drafts. This evaluation may lead to a need for more planning and drafting as he revises and edits the blog post. When Lee reaches a point where his writing is finished, it is time for him to submit the post. He should do one last review to correct any errors and improve the formatting, and then he can publish the post on his blog. A blog allows Lee to continue to revise his work, respond to others' comments, and write follow-up posts, so Lee might choose to continue the writing process even after his blog post is published.

The following is an example of an **ineffective** response. It contains some language errors, such as inconsistent verb tense, and vague ideas. Get some extra practice by revising the following response.

The writing process can help Lee write a better blog post. First, he can start with planning. When he skipped the planning stage, he ran out of ideas. During planning, he could brainstorm ideas for the body, introduction, and conclusion. Lee went straight to the drafting stage. If Lee started with planning, drafting will be easier. He can create a central idea and outline, which he will use for drafting. As Lee writes and after he writes, he should evaluate his writing. This would give him ideas for revising. When he is satisfied with his blog post, he can check for errors and then publish the post on his blog.

2. The following is an example of an **effective** response. It clearly summarizes the argument in the passage and evaluates it using specific evidence.

The 1875 Supreme Court of Wisconsin had a backwards view of women. Its argument against allowing women to practice law in the Court was that women must be protected and not exposed to real-world problems. However, women live in the real world. Duer Miller makes this point by noting that the Court mentioned three crimes against women as too horrific for female lawyers to address. If a woman is abused or raped, should it fall to only men to decide on the consequences of that crime? If a woman is victimized, is it "reverence" and "faith" to stop women from talking about that crime and advocating for better treatment? Disallowing women from the courtroom by "protecting" them means that women receive no voice in crimes committed against them. Duer Miller's argument is compelling and convincing.

The following is an example of an **ineffective** response. The writer's reasoning is unclear and lacking specifics. Get some extra practice by revising the following response to better support its position.

Duer Miller's implied argument is that the Supreme Court demeaned women by trying to protect them. This is a poor argument in favor of women being able to argue in front of the court. The Supreme Court of Wisconsin ruled that women could not practice law in front of the court, so that is their ruling. Since this is a Supreme Court ruling, it was a good argument.

Women don't have to argue in front of a court. That is a way that women don't always have to have the same jobs as men. It doesn't mean women aren't as good as men, the court respects them. Overall, Duer Miller's argument is not convincing.

Organization   *page 13*

Organizing Short Answers   *page 15*

Organizing a Short Answer Using the Writing Process

Practice It!   *pages 20–23*

1a. **Central Idea:** In a study on the effect of regular exercise on clinical depression, a control group would not exercise regularly so that scientists could more accurately measure the effects of exercise.

Details: A control group is not affected by the factor being studied. Comparing the experimental group to a control group allows scientists to effectively test an independent variable. An experiment with a control group can account for complex factors that might affect the experimental group.

1b. You might write:

Beginning:

A study on the effect of regular exercise on clinical depression should include a control group that does not follow a regular exercise routine so that scientists can more accurately measure the effects of exercise.

Middle:

A well-designed study uses an experimental group and a control group. The control group is not affected by the factor being studied, the independent variable. In this case, the independent variable is regular exercise. Comparing the experimental group to a control group allows scientists to effectively test the independent variable. In a study on the effect of regular exercise on clinical depression, scientists should compare changes in clinical depression among the control group (which does not get regular exercise) with changes among the experimental group (which does get regular exercise). An experiment with a control group can account for complex factors that might affect the experimental group, such as changes in environment or life events that might affect depression.

Ending:

If scientists designed a study that only tracked depressed individuals who took regular exercise, they might find that 25% of those individuals experienced improvement in their depression. But what does that number mean? If a control group showed 5% improvement, the study's results would be far different than if a control group showed 25% improvement also. The control group gives the study context.

2a. Central Idea: Based on the Doscero Industries company policy, Kara should report her concerns to her manager's supervisor.

Details: "Doscero Industries encourages an open environment where employees can voice their ideas and concerns." "If a concern involves the manager's performance directly, the employee should voice this concern to the manager's superior." "The company will act promptly to respond to improper behavior and will not tolerate any retaliation."

2b. You might write:

Beginning:

Based on the Doscero Industries company policy, Kara should report her concerns to her manager's supervisor.

Middle:

The company professes to want employees to voice their concerns, stating that it "encourages an open environment." Certainly, the company's official position is that Kara should communicate her ethical concern that her boss is favoring another employee. Since the issue directly involves her manager, according to the policy, Kara should contact her manager's supervisor. By writing an email to the supervisor and including references to the employee manual, she can maintain documentation of her complaint and her compliance with company policy. Kara might be concerned about retaliation from her manager, but the manual clearly states that the company "will not tolerate any retaliation."

Ending:

Any employee who has an ethical concern about a direct superior is in a difficult position, but the Doscero Industries company policy gives Kara a clear course of action to address the situation.

You can use some direct quotes in your response, but don't rely on them. Restate ideas from the passage to show that you understand.

Check Your Skills *pages 24–26*

1. The following is an example of an **effective** response. The beginning explains the amplified greenhouse effect. The middle identifies the arguments for reduced growth in the future and evaluates those arguments. The ending makes a big-picture observation about the results of climate change.

According to NASA, scientists have identified a phenomenon, known as the amplified greenhouse effect, that is changing the growing season and amount of vegetation in northern latitudes. The reduction of polar ice and snow increases the greenhouse effect, causing increased warming in northern areas and more green growth. The article presents an argument that increased plant growth may not continue. First, side effects of growth such as forest fires and drought may slow growth. Second, availability of water and sunlight may limit growth of plant life. These arguments are logical, since these are well known and clearly observable factors that affect plant growth in other areas. The article does not provide data about forest fires, infestations, drought, and available resources for plant growth, so it seems that there are many unknown factors affecting the potential future landscape of northern areas. Ecosystems are complex, and while we can observe current warming trends and changes in seasonal growth, the long-term effects of climate change are not as easy to predict.

The following is an example of an **ineffective** response. It includes some poor word choices (i.e., "the idea of the amplified greenhouse effect" instead of simply "the amplified greenhouse effect," "ground" instead of "Earth") and fails to evaluate the arguments the article gives for why plant growth might not continue to increase. For extra practice, try revising this response.

The idea of the amplified greenhouse effect occurs through the interaction of gases such as carbon dioxide that trap the heat against the ground, causing polar ice and snow to melt. Although trees are already growing where there was once snow, scientists report that the increase in plants might not continue the same. Ironically, the warming effect that is causing the increase in plant life is likely to have negative effects, such as forest fires and droughts, that will stop more plant growth. While the northern latitudes may become warmer and lose their ice pack, they may not be as green as we would expect.

2. The following is an example of an **effective** response. It includes details from the article that explain why arctic and antarctic ice is expected to melt.

The greenhouse effect causes warming of the Earth because of gasses and clouds in the atmosphere. An increasing greenhouse effect is projected to cause ice melt in the arctic and antarctic. The diagram of the greenhouse effect shows that radiation from the sun is either absorbed by the Earth or reflected into the atmosphere. Some of the reflected radiation is trapped as heat by clouds and gasses in the atmosphere. According to the article, increased water vapor, carbon dioxide, and methane trap heat near the Earth's surface. This causes ice to melt in both northern and southern latitudes, affecting arctic and antarctic ice. Once ice and snow has melted, the article notes that the exposed land and ocean is less reflective. More heat is absorbed by the Earth, and this also causes increased warming and, in turn, more ice melt. The factors limiting plant growth do not limit ice melt, which may continue as long as the Earth continues to warm.

The following is an example of an **ineffective** response. It is repetitive, lacks good organization, and relies on a long quote from the article without explaining it or expanding on it. For extra practice, try revising this response.

The greenhouse effect is a way that the Earth is getting warmer, and because the Earth is getting warmer, ice will melt. Ice melts in warm temperatures. The article says that "increased concentrations of heat-trapping gasses, such as water vapor, carbon dioxide, and methane, cause Earth's surface, ocean, and lower atmosphere to warm." The sun shines on the Earth, and it makes the Earth warm. Some of the warmth gets trapped because of "clouds, carbon dioxide, and other gasses." This means the arctic and antarctic ice will both melt.

3. The following is an example of an **effective** response. It includes details from the passage as well as evaluations and responses to the arguments in the passage. It makes original arguments in favor of the proposed bill.

Dear Senator:

I am writing in opposition to the proposed bill to cut military spending over the next five years. The Department of Defense is especially crucial in a time of instability in many parts of the world, including the Middle East. I understand that proponents of this bill note that China and Russia spend only $150 billion annually on their militaries, but the amount of military spending of other countries does not necessarily indicate our military need. The United States military has been overextended through conflicts in the Middle East, so clearly our military is not too large. Opponents of the bill note that Medicare, Medicaid, and Social Security make up a larger percentage of the budget than military spending. While this does not necessarily mean that these programs should be cut instead of the Department of Defense budget, it shows that there are other parts of the budget to examine for potential spending reduction. I strongly encourage you to vote against the proposed bill.

Sincerely,

A Concerned Taxpayer

The following is an example of an **ineffective** response. It gives little information and does not critique the argument from the passage in any way. It does not acknowledge the opposing arguments. For extra practice, try revising this response.

Dear Senator:

I am writing in favor of the proposed bill to cut military spending over the next five years. I hope you vote in favor of it! I discovered that our military spending is more than four times China and Russia combined! That is an unbelievable statistic. Why are we spending so much money on defense? Please vote in favor of this reasonable bill to cut unreasonable spending.

Sincerely,

A Concerned Taxpayer

Organizing Extended Responses *page 27*

Developing an Organized Extended Response
Practice It!   *pages 32–35*

1a.

Central Idea:	Details or Explanation:
Jefferson said institutions must "keep pace with the times," and the changing times require that the Constitution be amended to limit the powers of corporations.	The Founding Fathers likely never foresaw corporations to be considered as "citizens" with rights.

Supporting Idea:	Details and Evidence:
Corporations are not citizens.	"inhuman, legal entities without inherent rights" vs. "associations of citizens"
	The Supreme Court considers corporations "associations of citizens." Corporations are not citizens in other ways, i.e. going to jail, voting.
Supporting idea:	**Details and Evidence:**
A constitutional amendment is needed because the Supreme Court made the ruling that corporations deserve free speech.	The Supreme Court rules on constitutionality, so only a constitutional amendment can counter the ruling.
	Jefferson: "new discoveries are made, new truths disclosed" Citizens United is a new way of looking at corporations.
Conclusion:	**Details or Explanation:**
Changing the Constitution is not a light decision.	Citizens United immediately/significantly affected elections, so a constitutional amendment is worth pursuing.

1b. You might write:

Jefferson professed that institutions must "keep pace with the times," and the changing times require that the Constitution be amended to limit the powers of corporations. Mr. Kittridge makes a strong argument that it is wrong to assign corporations rights. The Founding Fathers likely never foresaw that corporations might be considered citizens, and so a constitutional amendment is appropriate to adapt to unforeseen changes in society.

Mr. Kittridge makes the argument that corporations are not citizens and should not have rights. His position is in opposition to the Supreme Court decision that classifies corporations as "associations of citizens." While groups of private citizens certainly have the same rights as individuals to freedom of speech and assembly, a corporation is clearly not merely a group of citizens. As Kittridge points out, a corporation is a legal entity that protects owners from business liabilities. The purpose of a corporation is to conduct business and make money, and so a corporation has self-interest to promote. However, that same corporation has no empathy, civic duty, or personal liability. Defining a corporation as an "association of citizens" with human rights is misguided at best.

A constitutional amendment is needed because the Supreme Court made the ruling that corporations deserve free speech. The Supreme Court rules on constitutionality, so clarifying the Constitution with an amendment seems the best way to counter the Citizens United decision. Jefferson said that changes in government are needed when "new discoveries are made, new truths disclosed." Modern corporations are a new truth in society, and the government needs rules that clearly define corporations as different from individuals.

Changing the Constitution is not a light decision, and Jefferson points out that "frequent and untried" changes could be hazards to government. Citizens United immediately and significantly affected elections with an influx of financial contributions, so it requires a strong response. A constitutional amendment defining corporations as entities without rights meets Jefferson's criteria for necessary change.

1c. When you evaluate your work, look for strong organization, with supporting ideas clarified by strong details and evidence.

2a.

Central Idea:	Details or Explanation:
The arguments against zero-tolerance policies are stronger.	Zero-tolerance policies try to eliminate problems with biased decision making or student excuses, but the problems they cause are serious.
Supporting Idea:	**Details and Evidence:**
Zero-tolerance policies attempt to deal with real problems, but they cause serious issues.	Witness reports are unreliable, and teachers can be biased.
	"Zero-tolerance" creates unfair circumstances, i.e. expulsion for minor offences. Victims may be punished along with bullies.

Answers and Explanations

Supporting idea:	Details and Evidence:
The best way of dealing with violence is not necessarily expulsion or suspension.	Violence doesn't go away when students are kicked out of school. Violence signifies emotional, psychological problems.
Conclusion:	Details or Explanation:
The idea of the punishment fitting the crime is an important one.	Treating all situations with one broad-stroke solution rarely works. Each circumstance needs an appropriate response.

2b. You might write:

It is easy to understand how a zero-tolerance policy might be appealing. Any of us might, in a moment of frustration, cry, "Why would they allow violent students in our schools?" Zero-tolerance policies attempt to increase safety and security while eliminating problems with biased decision-making. However, the arguments against such policies are stronger. Zero-tolerance policies cause serious problems, and it is questionable whether they provide effective solutions.

Zero-tolerance policies address real issues of teacher or administrator bias, unreliable witness reports, and student lies. Addressing each conflict on its own merits is a difficult task. If punishments could be reliably automated to eliminate human error, it might be a good thing. A zero-tolerance policy, however, does not dole out punishments well. Bullied students may be punished for defending themselves or even simply for being attacked. Instances of unfair expulsion or suspension are worse than potential bias in punishment. They rob students of their education.

The best way of dealing with violence is not necessarily expulsion or suspension. As opponents of zero-tolerance policies note, violence is merely pushed out of the school, not properly addressed. Violence signifies emotional, psychological, social, or even physical problems. Students involved in violent instances need help more than expulsion. An important piece of evidence is missing from the proponents' arguments for zero-tolerance policies: evidence that the policies are effective in reducing violence and improving education. On the other hand, there is evidence that students can be hurt unfairly by these policies.

The idea of the punishment fitting the crime is an important one, and treating all situations with one

broad-stroke solution rarely works. Each circumstance is different and needs an appropriate response to help both the instigators and victims of violence.

2c. When you evaluate your work, look for strong organization, with supporting ideas clarified by strong details and evidence.

Check Your Skills

1. The following is an example of an **effective** response. It addresses and evaluates the arguments in the passage, and it has a clear position.

Based on the positions stated in the passage, the evidence in favor of banning or regulating energy drinks is strongest. Those in favor of regulation have strong evidence of harmful health effects, and arguments against regulation ignore those hazards.

Serious health effects such as convulsion, anaphylactic shock, and even death have been documented by the Food and Drug Administration, a reliable source. The example of the high school student who suffered a seizure and nearly died as the result of consuming an energy drink brings this threat home. Any teen could suffer the same reaction. Can these drinks be considered safe? The additional reports of energy drinks harming pregnant women are also significant. The proponents of energy drinks categorize them as healthy, noting ingredients such as antioxidants and herbal remedies. This makes the drinks even more dangerous. Children, teens, and pregnant women are likely unaware of the risks.

The arguments against regulation in this passage fail to take into account the health risks of energy drinks. Comparing regulating energy drinks to anti-tobacco campaigns invites a comparison. Both products are harmful, and both need regulation. Both are represented by companies with a financial interest, and those companies will fight regulation on every level. Energy drink proponents state that the risk of death from an energy drink is less than risk of death from cigarettes. The argument is that energy drinks are not risky enough to ban, but the risks the FDA has compiled include death and miscarriage. Should the "free market" be free to advertise products as healthy when they could cause death?

The controversy should not be over whether to regulate products with proven health risks. The controversy should be over how to regulate those products. At a minimum, consumers need to be aware of the risks associated with energy drinks.

The following is an example of an **ineffective** response. It does not have enough specific details and a clear progression of ideas. It does use the passage to construct an argument, but it needs better organization and clearer support. Try revising this response for extra practice.

Energy drinks aren't good for you, and so banning them is probably a good idea. The idea of something giving you a seizure is really bad and harmful. Companies will always want to advertise their products, and they aren't the ones who are going to tell you that something is bad for you. Like the passage says, banning energy drinks is like banning tobacco. Maybe tobacco is worse, but both are being banned for the same reasons. Both have health hazards. Energy drinks can cause seizures, miscarriages, and death. Tobacco can cause lung cancer, emphysema, and death. Under 18-years-old shouldn't be able to buy either one. We can trust the FDA to say what's good for us, and it's pretty obvious that energy drinks aren't.

2. The following is an example of an **effective** response. It has a clear and well-supported position.

A regulation banning energy drinks with more than 100 milligrams of caffeine per serving is a better choice than a regulation preventing anyone under 18 from buying energy drinks. The problems with energy drinks are better addressed by attacking the source of the problem: excessive caffeine in the drinks.

The health dangers from energy drinks are due to high levels of caffeine. The dangers aren't limited to teenagers and children. Pregnant women are at particular risk, since fetal distress syndrome and miscarriage are possible hazards. A ban on high-caffeine energy drinks would help address these significant dangers.

A regulation banning higher-caffeine energy drinks is also easier to enforce. Alcohol and cigarettes, though illegal for teens, are still accessible. Limiting caffeine levels of drinks is enforceable at the level of the manufacturer, distributor, and retailer. Businesses already must deal with regulations for safety. Adding this additional regulation is not an undue burden and benefits the health of the community.

The manufacturer is the one most responsible for the hazards of high-caffeine drinks. It makes sense to require manufacturers to reduce caffeine levels or stop selling their drinks. No consumer needs a drink with more than 100 milligrams of caffeine per serving. A ban on high-caffeine drinks is a sensible solution.

The following is an example of an **ineffective** response. It does not choose a clear position, although it does address some arguments for each regulation. It needs more development and a strong central idea. This response also includes casual and indecisive language, such as "I guess." Try revising this response for extra practice.

A regulation banning high-caffeine drinks might be a good idea, or stopping teenagers from buying high-caffeine drinks might be a good idea too. If you don't have high-caffeine drinks available to buy, you won't buy as much caffeine. But I guess you could buy a lot of drinks at once and still get a lot of caffeine. That might be kind of dangerous. If you don't let kids buy energy drinks, they wouldn't drink them. Pregnant ladies or adults could still have seizures, miscarriages, or other health problems from too much caffeine. That's also a problem but maybe not the one the regulations are trying to solve. If you had both regulations, then you would have less danger of people having "caffeine toxicity" like it says in the passage. I guess I would be in favor of either of the regulations being put in place.

Developing Ideas, Arguments, and Evidence page 39

Developing Ideas page 41

Expand Your Ideas

Practice It! pages 44–46

1. **Central Idea:** The argument to fund NASA is stronger.

   Supporting Ideas: Space exploration helps with social problems because of technology development. Space exploration is not excessively expensive.

   Details: 0.6% of budget; "intangible benefits"; solar panels; heart monitors; water-purification systems

2. You might write:

   The argument of NASA supporters is stronger than the argument to defund the space agency. The argument's strength lies in its refutation of the idea that space exploration does not contribute to solving real-world problems. Space exploration does help with social problems because it promotes technological development. Far from having only "intangible benefits," space exploration has given us solar panels

Answers and Explanations

that may provide cheap, accessible energy and heart monitors that can reduce long-term health care costs. Water-purification systems can provide fresh water to third-world countries and rural areas. It is short-sighted to ignore these benefits, especially when space exploration is not excessively expensive. A budget of $18 billion may sound enormous until you realize that it is only 0.6% of the national budget. The wide-ranging benefits of solar panels, cancer therapy, and light-weight materials are worth the investment.

3. Evaluate the development of your ideas. Does your writing include related ideas? Does your writing make connections between your ideas and details?

4. **Central Idea:** The parasite D. medineses depends on hosts throughout its life cycle.

   Supporting Ideas: Larvae are eaten by copepods, which transfer them to human hosts. Larvae infest humans and grow to maturity in human hosts.

   Details: Larvae infect humans through water containing infested copepods. Larvae grow in stomach and intestine walls. Roundworms mature and mate in humans, and males die there. Female roundworms create and emerge through a blister, usually in the foot. Copepods eat larvae, which develop in them until they can infect humans.

5. You might write:

   The parasite D. medineses, known as roundworm, depends on two hosts throughout its life cycle: copepods and humans. Larvae are eaten by copepods, which transfer the larvae to human hosts. The immature roundworms are dependent on copepods for an environment where the larvae can develop until they can infect humans. Then the larvae are transported into humans through water containing infested copepods. Roundworms are dependent on human hosts through the rest of their life cycles. The larvae grow in human stomach walls and intestine walls. Roundworms mature and mate in humans, and males die there. Female roundworms use human hosts to transport their larvae to copepods by creating and emerging through a blister, usually in the foot. There is no point when a roundworm is not dependent on a host, except for the brief period when released larvae wait to be ingested by copepods.

Check Your Skills

1. The following is an example of an **effective** response. It contains supporting ideas and specific details from the passage that develop the central idea.

   The arguments in the passage supporting a minimum wage increase are stronger than those opposing it. The opposing arguments seem logical. However, they include no hard evidence to support their logic. To argue an economic issue, specific evidence and economic studies are essential.

   The opposing arguments in the passage rely entirely on logical reasoning about what might happen. Opponents say that businesses would hire fewer workers but do not present evidence of this behavior in the past. The claim that a minimum wage increase would cause increased prices is logical, but it would be a much stronger claim with specific evidence linking wages and price increases.

   The passage also presents logical arguments supporting a minimum wage increase. The argument that minimum wage earners will spend their additional income, fueling the economy, is logical. The difference is that this argument is backed by evidence from an economic study by the Federal Reserve Bank of Chicago. Supporters also compare the current minimum wage to the current federal poverty level, which puts the wage level in objective perspective.

   The presented arguments against the minimum wage increase could be compelling, but because the passage lacks concrete evidence for these arguments, the arguments in favor of the minimum wage are stronger. Speculating about economic issues is problematic, since economics is a complex field. Hard evidence based on scientific study is needed.

   The following is an example of an **ineffective** response. It has a strong central idea and some supporting ideas, but it does not develop its ideas. It lacks details. Practice your writing skills by rewriting and editing this response to improve it.

   The arguments in the passage that oppose minimum wage increases are stronger. The opponents to minimum wage increases present more arguments, and the arguments are based in strong logic. It is obvious that minimum wage increases will cause problems for businesses and consumers. The supporting arguments have some evidence in their favor, but it is unlikely that a minimum wage increase will actually spur the economy. The arguments opposing minimum wage will cancel out any benefits mentioned in the arguments supporting a minimum wage increase.

Overall, it is clear that an increase in the minimum wage would be bad for economic growth. A minimum wage increase is a bad idea.

2. The following is an example of an **effective** response. It demonstrates how both arguments presented in the passage reflect King's quotation. The ideas are developed with details.

By using terms such as "spiritual death," "revolution of values," and "social vision," King puts his emphasis on moral values. Though the passage tackles the economics of minimum wage increase, both positions include moral arguments.

The argument in favor of a minimum wage increase echoes King's position, which calls for an "adequate wage" for every American. Comparing the minimum wage to the poverty level highlights the value-based foundation of the argument. The call for a "living wage" is a call for social equity.

The opposing argument also presents a value-based argument. The claim that the poor would be hurt most by a minimum wage increase is based in social values. Lost jobs and increased prices are long-term concerns. If those harms outweigh the benefits of a minimum wage, then the socially responsible position is to oppose minimum wage increases.

King's focus on social values is reflected in both arguments. The question is not whether our nation should pursue policies that help lift families out of poverty but how to define those policies.

The following is an example of an **ineffective** response. It lacks specific details that develop the ideas. Try revising and editing this response to improve it.

In the quotation, Martin Luther King, Jr. focuses on social values, while the passage about minimum wage increases weighs both economic and value-based arguments. Both arguments touch on social values. The argument in favor of a minimum wage increase asks for the same thing as King does, a living wage. However, the argument against a minimum wage increase argues that minimum wages hurt the poor in the long run. It takes the position that long-term effects are just as important as immediate benefits. The social benefits and costs of any policy need to be examined carefully.

Developing Strong Support   *page 49*

STAR Support

Practice It!   *pages 53–54*

1. c. The movie theater used to show a double feature every Saturday night.

   This answer does not describe a benefit of renovating the movie theater or a desire to renovate the theater.

2. a. How renovating drive-in theaters has spurred economic growth in similar towns

   Facts about economic growth in a similar situation would support the developer's case that renovating the theater would spur economic growth.

3a. The only fact that the argument includes is that the theater caused traffic in the 1980s. This fact is not very specific. It doesn't have information about how bad the traffic was and what caused it, specifically. Other statements are very general. The idea that the theater would encourage underage drinking seems to be speculation. The lack of specific facts makes the argument less convincing.

3b. The only fact that the argument includes is about traffic in the 1980s. Many things could have changed in recent years, such as expanded roads or nearby construction. The lack of timely evidence makes the argument less convincing.

3c. The accuracy of the facts is difficult to judge. There is no source given for the increased traffic in the 1980s. The idea that teens will drink in their cars is unsupported. The idea that it is unfair for taxpayers to pay for business development is opinion. The lack of clearly accurate facts makes the argument less convincing.

3d. The facts that the argument provides are relevant, but there are too few well-supported facts to make a convincing argument. Traffic, potential drinking, and costs to taxpayers are all relevant issues. The arguments are only weakened by the lack of specific, timely, and accurate evidence.

4a. The best example of specific evidence in the passage is the example of two people who were severely injured walking along the shoulder of the road. This example shows that the danger of walking on a road without sidewalks is real. Statistics comparing injuries on streets with and without sidewalks would be better evidence, however, since statistical evidence is more reliable than the anecdotal evidence of individual stories. A combination of statistical and anecdotal evidence is often the most convincing.

4b. One sentence that is irrelevant is, "We require bicyclists to wear helmets; we should have roads with sidewalks." Requiring helmets for bicyclists is not clearly analogous to installing sidewalks.

4c. One statement with questionable accuracy is, "Our citizens should not be afraid to walk to the park or the grocery store." There is no evidence in the passage that citizens are afraid to walk. Another statement of questionable accuracy is that the benefits of sidewalks outweigh the costs. The author does not provide information about the costs of sidewalks, and there is no way to compare costs and benefits.

5. You might write:

The argument in the passage is somewhat supported. It provides specific evidence of some injuries to pedestrians walking on streets without sidewalks. The anecdotal example in the passage is recent and relevant. Its accuracy could be checked. The argument also includes some questionable statements, such as that citizens are afraid to walk the streets. The author's argument would be better supported by statistics about the number of accidents on roads with and without sidewalks as well as by facts about the costs of installing sidewalks.

Check Your Skills   *pages 55–56*

1. The following is an example of an **effective** response. It uses STAR Support to evaluate the arguments in each passage.

The passage that supports privatization of national parks has stronger evidence, but both passages lack specific examples or data to support their argument. The passage supporting privatization has stronger evidence because it cites more comprehensive and valid evidence than the opposing passage.

The passage supporting government-run national parks has little evidence and relies mainly on general statements of opinion. It does state that privatization in the past has resulted in less public access at greater cost. Since this evidence specifically relates to national parks, it could be strong evidence. However, the author does not mention where and when this happened. Its timeliness and accuracy is unknown.

The opposing passage states that private business is more efficient in running telephone services and utilities, but it also fails to give specific examples comparing government-run utilities to privately-run ones. The passage also cites mismanagement of parks by government. It gives some specifics, such as understaffing and roads in disrepair. However, this evidence could be much more specific. How many parks are currently understaffed? Where and when were visitors endangered? The author only states that his examples are from the 20th century. A 100-year timeframe can't be considered timely. Finally, the passage states that industry outperforms government in creating vacation destinations. This statement also lacks specific evidence, although destinations such as Disneyland or Las Vegas come to mind. How do these private destinations compare to the Grand Canyon or Yellowstone?

Although both passages lack specific evidence, the second passage provides more relevant specifics than the first. To ultimately determine which position is better policy, it would be necessary to examine specific evidence of privately-run versus publicly-run parks, utilities, and vacation destinations.

The following is an example of an **ineffective** response. It doesn't clearly address the arguments in the passages. Try revising and editing this response for extra practice.

Definitely, parks should be supported by the government. If the parks are understaffed, it's because the government isn't funding them with enough money. On the other hand, what are companies going to do with parks? They just want to make money, and they'll definitely charge more money, build on land that should be preserved, and cause us ultimately lose control of public lands. Who knows? Maybe they'll start logging in Yellowstone and build casinos in the Grand Canyon. That's not a good road to follow.

Evaluating Arguments   *page 57*

Describe the Claim, Evidence, and Speaker

Learn It!   *page 60*

4. You might write:

The author makes a clear claim that two years of college education should be free to U.S. students. The claim is somewhat reasonable. The government provides many services and could expand public education by two years. However, this would incur significant costs and changes in the educational system, and the author's support is weak. One piece of evidence that is specific, timely, accurate, and relevant is that over 60% of jobs will require degrees by 2018. Other statements in the passage are vague, such as the idea that students would quickly decide on majors. This idea isn't supported by specifics and seems mainly to be speculation. It has no source. The statement that college graduates often cannot find jobs undermines the idea that two years of free college is a solution. Overall, the evidence seems insufficient, especially since it does not address the costs of the proposal. The author acknowledges that opposition exists but does not address any counterarguments.

Practice It!

pages 61–62

1. The claim that holiday parades are a waste of resources is clear. It is stated in the first sentence. It is a reasonable claim, depending mainly on a value judgment, since the benefits of parades (such as a sense of community) are difficult to quantify.

2. The evidence in the first paragraph, which states that there are possible alternatives to parades, is somewhat irrelevant. Why are other events less wasteful? The evidence in the passage includes some examples of negative results of parades: traffic, trash, and expenses for police. The evidence would be more specific if the author provided total costs for various parades. The timeliness and source of the evidence is unknown, since the evidence is not very specific.

3. The speaker is unknown, and the lack of specific evidence indicates that the speaker is not an expert. However, the speaker does acknowledge an opposing viewpoint, mentioning that parades are festive and happy.

4. You might write:

The argument in the passage has some strengths, but it lacks specific and compelling evidence. The claim is clear and reasonable: that holiday parades are wasteful. The speaker acknowledges that parades are festive and happy and suggests alternatives. However, simply suggesting that there are alternatives to parades does not make a clear argument for the claim. Other events substituted for parades may be as costly as parades. The evidence that parades block traffic, create trash, and require overtime from city workers is logical. However, it is not specific. How much do parades cost? How much waste do they produce? How detrimental are the effects on traffic? Without more specific and relevant support, the overall argument is weak.

5. The claim in the passage is clear: that the U.S. should allow driverless cars in every state. It is a reasonable claim, since some states already have such laws.

6. The evidence in the passage generally provides specific, timely, accurate, and relevant details. The author mentions states that have laws allowing driverless cars. This would be more relevant if the author explicitly explained the results of these laws. However, the author does give examples of the safety and successful testing of driverless cars. Driverless cars have navigated Lombard Street and traveled 300,000 miles with only one accident, caused by another car. These details would be more compelling if the author included a source. The author does mention a 2012 video posted by Google, showing a blind man using a driverless car. This evidence is specific and timely. Google as a company is interested in promoting self-driving cars, but there does not seem to be a strong reason to doubt the story in the video and the benefits of driverless cars to the disabled.

7. The speaker in the passage is unknown. The speaker does provide some specific details that show knowledge of the subject. However, the speaker does not acknowledge any potential counterarguments.

8. You might write:

The passage provides a strong argument in favor of legalizing self-driving cars. The speaker clearly states the claim and provides detailed evidence. Several states already have laws allowing driverless cars, and although the author does not explain the results of these laws, he or she does give details about tests of self-driving cars. After 300,000 miles of testing with only one accident, caused by another car, driverless cars seem safe. The author also gives an example of an blind man using a driverless car. This example shows the benefits of self-driving cars. The argument could be improved by addressing possible counterarguments, but overall, it makes a strong case for a clear claim.

Check Your Skills

pages 63–64

1. The following is an example of an **effective** response. It evaluates each passage, noting positive and negative aspects, and makes a clear judgment about which gives the stronger argument.

The passage opposing royalty makes a stronger case against this outdated custom. The passage supporting royalty includes specific evidence. However, when its evidence is weighed against the serious issues that a royal class poses for a society, the evidence seems less relevant and compelling.

The author who argues in favor of royalty makes a clear claim: that royalty should be preserved. The example of Great Britain is a good one. The constitutional monarchy provides a parliamentary democracy while maintaining a royal family. The author's evidence primarily revolves around the popularity of British royalty. Millions watched the marriage of Prince Charles and Lady Diana, and while this example is not very current, the recent birth of Prince George shows the ongoing popularity of the royal family. However, the popularity of royal events is rather frivolous. The author does not address counterarguments, and this is very detrimental to the pro-royalty position. After all, what was the cost of Charles and Diana's royal wedding?

The passage opposing royalty makes a stronger case. It has a clear claim: that royalty is anti-democratic. A monarchy is clearly a delineation of an upper-class by birth, and this goes against fundamental principles of democracy. The author quotes Graham Smith's writings on CNN. This quote points out that the royal family is not subject to Freedom of Information laws. It also puts a dollar amount, over two hundred million pounds a year, on the monarchy. These are weighty points that need to be addressed. The author's argument that a lack of royalty drives innovation and individuality is not well supported, but the problems with royalty are clearly stated.

When a royal family is no longer in complete political control, what is its value or detriment to society? The arguments in favor of royalty are about valuing culture and sharing popular cultural experiences. The arguments against royalty are concerned with secretive political influence, high expenses, and a lack of democratic equality. These arguments are stronger because they are significant and potentially damaging to society. Culture can still be preserved without preserving a royal class.

The following is an example of an **ineffective** response. It lacks good organization and a clear evaluation of each argument. Try revising this response for extra practice.

A royal family is okay to have if they do not make the laws. The first argument is that 750 million people watched Prince Charles and Lady Diana's wedding. That shows that lots of people like British royalty, and they don't care so much about the expenses. If people want something, why not give it to them. There is a good argument that culture is the benefit of royalty. When people in the U.S. want to read about royalty on the news all the time, that is showing that royalty fill a role that people want. If people want something, then you shouldn't try to take it away from them.

The main thing is, does royalty actually cause problems? We pay for lots of things just because people

enjoy them. Cities build football stadiums because people like football. What's the harm in having a royal family so that people can have something they enjoy? The dresses at big events are nice and something every girl dreams of when she is little. Why can't there be a little bit of culture that people will like?

After looking at the evidence, it's good to see that it's okay to have a royal family. People in Britain still vote and have a legislature just like the U.S. Everyone can enjoy their royal families and watch them on TV. It's not hurting anyone, so it's okay.

Citing Evidence and Connecting with Claims   *page 65*

Building a Chain of Evidence

Learn It!   *page 67*

5. You might write:

I recommend interviewing Angela Goren for the sales position because of her familiarity with the company and her success in sales. In her last position, Angela received a promotion after six months, which demonstrates her success in sales. She also may need less training, since she is already familiar with the company's products. In addition, Angela has a BA in communications. Because of this, she may have good communications skills that will help her show clients the benefits of our products. Angela is the most promising candidate.

Practice It!   *pages 68–70*

1a. The argument that wet conditions were created by impact events is more logical.

1b. There were obvious impactors in the past. In CO_2 atmospheres, greenhouse potential is limited by clouds, and no carbonate has been detected. Methane requires a source. SO_2 may not build up to high enough levels.

1c. Because there are clear indications of large impactors in the past, there is evidence for impact events that may have caused a wet climate.

There is no evidence for CO_2 as the cause, since no carbonate has been detected, and clouds in CO_2 atmospheres makes this explanation less likely.

With no known source of methane, the idea that methane is the cause lacks evidence.

The cause is unlikely to be SO_2 since there is no evidence the levels would have been high enough.

1d. Since three pieces of evidence have to do with the composition of Mars's atmosphere and the lack of evidence for hypotheses that focus on atmospheric composition, it is logical to group them together. You might start with your claim, and then discuss the evidence in favor of impact events. Then, you could discuss all three atmospheric gasses together.

2. You might write:

The passage gives two potential reasons that early conditions on Mars were warm and wet: the atmospheric composition and large impact events. Of these two potential reasons, impact events seem more likely, given the information in the passage. There is evidence supporting the existence of large impacts in the past. In fact, the passage calls these impacts "obvious." This is the only positive evidence in the passage.

There is no evidence in the passage that methane, CO_2, or SO_2 might have caused a warm and wet climate in Mars's past. All three gasses pose problems. No carbonate has been detected that would support the existence of large amounts of carbon dioxide, and CO_2 would form clouds limiting its warming effects. Since there are no known source of methane on Mars, the idea that methane is the cause lacks evidence. The cause is also unlikely to be SO_2 since there is no evidence the levels would have been high enough. Impact events are the only proposed reason for Mars's early climate that have any supporting evidence in the passage.

3. Evaluate your claim and evidence. Is the evidence clearly connected to the claim?

4a. Claim: The argument against removing drink machines from schools is stronger.

Evidence: When all sugary drinks were banned, students still consumed the same amount.

The objective of removing soda machines is to combat childhood obesity.

4b. Because banning sugary drinks did not result in lower consumption, the policy is not effective.

There is evidence that sugary drinks contribute to obesity, but there is no evidence in the passage that banning them from schools reduces obesity.

4c. You might start with the claim, and then discuss the evidence that banning sugary drinks does not lower

obesity. Then you would end by pointing out that reducing obesity is the goal, and that the evidence doesn't show a resulting lower obesity.

5. You might write:

Since sugared drinks provide empty calories, it might seem logical that schools shouldn't serve them to students. However, the argument presented against banning sugary drinks is stronger. The study cited in the passage found that when all sugary drinks were banned from schools, students still drank the same amount of sugar. Because banning sugary drinks did not result in lower consumption, the policy is not effective. There is evidence that sugary drinks contribute to obesity, but there is no evidence in the passage that banning them from schools reduces obesity. Opponents of banning sugary drinks suggest health education as an alternative. If health education is more effective, then it is the policy that should be pursued.

Check Your Skills $\qquad$ *pages 71–72*

1. The following is an example of an **effective** response. It has a clear claim and makes connections between the evidence and the claim.

When businesses are in conflict, which businesses should government favor? Should ISPs be given freedom to control the information traveling over their service? Should websites be free from potential regulation or pressure from ISPs? The conflict over net neutrality highlights this issue, and the passage presents arguments both opposing and supporting net neutrality. Overall, the arguments in favor of net neutrality are stronger, although the passage leaves many questions unanswered.

The arguments supporting net neutrality are strong, but they are based on potential dangers of a lack of regulation. They would be stronger arguments if they were supported by evidence of these dangers, but the court ruling eliminating net neutrality rules is recent. It is prudent to consider the potential harms of eliminating regulation before deregulation creates damage.

Net neutrality prevents ISPs from controlling specific information that travels through the Internet. The arguments in the passage mention several ways ISPs could control information: by charging websites and web services, by banning or charging competitors, by blocking content for political reasons, or by banning negative commentary about their business. These are all examples of controlling and limiting information, infringing on individuals and businesses. Allowing ISPs to control information in these ways gives too much power to ISPs.

The arguments opposing net neutrality, on the other hand, favor deregulation for ISPs. The weakness of this argument is that it has a limited perspective. Deregulation can lead to innovation, but innovation and free-market growth do not make up for potentially dangerous abuses. If opponents do not address these abuses, the arguments against net neutrality are not convincing.

The Internet is a new and society-changing technology. It is difficult to make good choices regulating it. However, the potential costs of unregulated ISPs, as outlined in this passage, outweigh the potential benefits of deregulation.

The following is an example of an **ineffective** response. It lacks clear connections between the evidence and the claim. To practice your writing, try revising and editing this response to improve it.

Net neutrality is a good idea, and the arguments in favor of net neutrality are stronger. Those in favor of net neutrality put forth several reasons that net neutrality is a good policy. ISPs could charge websites so that people can access those websites if there is no net neutrality. Supporters of net neutrality also say that ISPs could block services or posts, while those against net neutrality mostly are in favor of freedom for ISPs. They want ISPs to have the ability to choose their business practices. Proponents of net neutrality counter that unregulated ISPs could interfere with the business practices of web services. Overall, net neutrality is a beneficial type of regulation.

2. The following is an example of an **effective** response. It makes a clear connection between the quotation and the passage, and it cites supporting evidence.

In the quotation, Thomas Jefferson outlines the limits and responsibilities of good government. He defines the purpose of government as stopping "men from injuring one another." Beyond that, government should give citizens freedom. The difficulty is in defining the line between protecting citizens from injury and abstaining from controlling and regulating. The passage on net neutrality illustrates the difficulty of defining this line.

The arguments in favor of net neutrality focus on protecting citizens from injury. Charging websites for bandwidth could result in limited access to services and limited competition. Blocking political content or criticisms of ISPs interferes with freedom of speech. Jefferson identifies protection from injury as the purview of government, but these are potential injuries.

How significant are they? Could they be curtailed with other regulations that would leave ISPs "free to regulate their own pursuits"?

On the other hand, opponents to net neutrality reflect Jefferson's concerns about government regulation. Opponents point out that free ISPs can make better decisions and manage Internet bandwidth. Jefferson says that the government should leave men free and able to enjoy the fruits of their labors. This is what ISPs will be able to do without the regulation of net neutrality. The better ISPs will benefit from their policies.

Both positions on net neutrality reflect different aspects of Jefferson's quotation. The conflict between them is a conflict between freedom from regulation and protection from injury, the two ideas in the quote from Jefferson.

The following is an example of an **ineffective** response. It makes a link between the quotation and the passage, but it lacks evidence from the passage. To practice your writing, try revising and editing this response to improve it.

The quotation from Jefferson argues in favor of a limited government that does not interfere with industry, and the arguments opposing net neutrality reflect this argument. Small government is a good idea because when individuals and business have more freedom, the result is a better marketplace. Competition creates better products and services. Jefferson advocates for a government that only focuses on preventing harm and lets each person work as he or she pleases and reap the rewards. The sentiment is pro-capitalist and anti-regulation. It supports many of the arguments opposing net neutrality.

Writing Practice   *page 73*

Practice for Reasoning through Language Arts   *page 75*

Comparing Arguments with the Writing Process

Practice It!   *pages 80–83*

1. Remember that you can write a response on either side of the issue. For extra practice, try writing two responses arguing for opposing points of view.

Central Idea: The arguments opposed to drilling in the Gulf of Mexico are stronger.	Explanation: The arguments against drilling include specifics and respond to arguments in favor of drilling.
Restate a Detail: Oil spills harm fishing and tourism.	Explanation: A main arguments for drilling is that it will create jobs, but an oil industry can also harm other industries.
Restate a Detail: The Deepwater Horizon spill in 2010 spilled millions of barrels.	Explanation: The argument against drilling gives a specific, recent example of harm.
Restate a Detail: Oil drilling is safer with modern technology.	Explanation: The argument in favor of drilling doesn't give any support for this statement.
Restate a Detail: There are two and a half years of oil reserves off shore.	Explanation: The quantity of oil is specific information, and the number of years of oil supply puts it in perspective.
Conclusion: The argument against drilling has more specific, convincing evidence.	Explanation: The argument in favor of drilling needs to address opposing arguments more thoroughly and include specific evidence.

2. You might write:

The passage opposing drilling in the Gulf of Mexico presents stronger arguments. Opponents to drilling cite specific evidence and respond to the arguments in favor of drilling. The arguments in favor of drilling have less specific support.

Opponents of drilling counter the claims of proponents. One of the main arguments in favor of drilling is that it will create jobs. However, opponents of drilling note that oil spills harm fishing and tourism. Harm to other industries should be considered in addition to the benefits of drilling.

The arguments against drilling also include specific details, including the Deepwater Horizon spill in 2010 that spilled millions of barrels. This is a specific, recent example of an harmful spill. It counters the argument that "with modern technology, oil can be drilled

safely." The argument in favor of drilling doesn't give any support for this statement. Another specific detail is the fact that there are approximately two and a half years of oil reserves off shore. The quantity of oil is specific information, and the number of years of oil supply puts it in perspective.

The argument against drilling has more specific, convincing evidence than the opposing argument. The argument in favor of drilling needs to address opposing arguments more thoroughly and include specific evidence in order to be convincing.

3. When you evaluate your work, check that the ideas and details are presented in a logical order. Make sure transitions are in place that connect your ideas. Your introduction and conclusion should make your central idea clear. Check for errors and edit for clarity.

4. Remember that you can write a response on either side of the issue. For extra practice, try writing two responses arguing for opposing points of view.

Central Idea: The arguments in favor of pet breeders are stronger.	Explanation: Those supporting pet breeders acknowledge problems, but also show the benefits of responsible breeding.
Restate a Detail: 40% of dogs are returned or abandoned.	Explanation: Specific evidence about the results of poor matches between dogs and owners
Restate a Detail: A lack of compatibility is the reason pets are abandoned.	Explanation: Breeders give owners predictable pets, and a good breeder can help match pets with owners.
Restate a Detail: Shelter animals have problems.	Explanation: While animals from breeders can have problems, so can animals from shelters.
Restate a Detail: Health problems occur in purebred dogs.	Explanation: Responsible breeders could limit health problems through good breeding practices.
Conclusion: The arguments show that breeders can benefit the broader community of pets and owners.	Explanation: The large numbers of animals in shelters show the need for breeders, since pets and owners need to be well matched.

5. You might write:

The passage presents strong arguments in favor of pet breeders. Supporters of pet breeders acknowledge problems but also show the benefits of responsible breeding. However, the opponents of pet breeders ignore the benefits of responsible breeding.

Proponents of breeders cite specific evidence. The fact that 40% of dogs are returned or abandoned within the first year shows the unfortunate results of poor matches between dogs and owners. A lack of compatibility is the reason many pets are abandoned, and this demonstrates that choosing compatible pets is important. Breeders give owners predictable pets with specific characteristics, and a good breeder can help match pets with owners.

Animals from both breeders and shelters can have problems. Shelter animals can have physical or emotional problems. They may have abandonment issues, or they may have been abused in the past. While health problems in purebred dogs are an issue, responsible breeders can limit health problems through good breeding practices.

The arguments in favor of breeders show that breeders can benefit the broader community of pets and owners. The large numbers of animals in shelters isn't a reason to remove breeders. These figures show the need for breeders, since pets and owners need to be well matched to avoid abandonment.

6. When you evaluate your work, check that the ideas and details are presented in a logical order. Make sure transitions are in place that connect your ideas. Your introduction and conclusion should make your central idea clear. Check for errors and edit for clarity.

Check Your Skills   *pages 84–86*

1. The following is an example of an **effective** response. It has a clear central idea, a strong introduction, a body with supporting ideas, and a clear conclusion.

Nuclear power is a much-debated source of energy. Both supporters and opponents of nuclear energy are concerned about the environment. Is nuclear power truly the key to a clean energy policy? Or do the dangers outweigh the costs? The passage opposing nuclear energy makes a strong argument that nuclear energy is too expensive and dangerous.

Perhaps the most controversial aspect of nuclear energy is the possibility of accidents. Supporters of nuclear energy dismiss disasters, stating that they are preventable. However, the fact that accidents are preventable doesn't mean they will be prevented. Humans are error-prone creatures. The recent disaster at the Fukushima nuclear plant shows that accidents can still happen. The costs are significant.

Both arguments also mention the cost of nuclear energy. The passage in support of nuclear power states that it is cheaper than wind, solar, or oil. It does not include details to support that statement, and the argument opposing nuclear power refutes it. The costs of storing waste and building power plants must be considered when weighing the affordability of nuclear energy.

With promising new technology arising for other types of energy, should nuclear power be pursued? Based on the arguments in the passages, less controversial sources of energy such as solar or geothermal power might be more promising investments.

The following is an example of an **ineffective** response. It has a clear central idea, but it is redundant. It summarizes the passage in favor of nuclear energy instead of analyzing the arguments. It doesn't address the arguments opposed to nuclear energy. To practice your writing, try revising and editing this response to improve it.

Nuclear energy is a good source of power that should be pursued. If nuclear energy can give us good power without downsides, there is no reason not to use it. Nuclear energy could be a big benefit. It is true that nuclear energy is clean energy that doesn't release carbon dioxide into the atmosphere. That means there is less pollution and harm to health. Nuclear energy helps us limit global warming. It also can be done without accidents or harm to the environment. Because nuclear power is cheap, it is a good source of energy. It should definitely be a kind of power that we use all the time.

2. The following is an example of an **effective** response. It has a clear central idea supported by evidence from the passage.

Texting while driving is clearly a dangerous activity. However, policies that make intuitive sense aren't always the best ones. The passage makes a strong argument opposing bans of texting behind the wheel.

The comparison between lowered speed limits and texting bans is apt. A law or regulation by itself won't stop a wide-spread behavior. Texting might be dangerous, but simply banning it won't solve the problem. The study that is cited in the passage shows that the policy is ineffective.

While long-term studies are worthwhile, their absence does not support a ban on texting. Neither do statistics showing the prevalence of texting while driving. The argument in favor of a ban on texting and driving

Essential Writing & Language Skills

rests almost entirely on statistics that show it is dangerous to text behind the wheel of a car. This is only an argument in favor of curbing dangerous texting. It is not an argument in favor of a specific policy or ban.

Bans on texting and driving deserve further study. Perhaps long-term studies will show that these bans eventually have effectiveness. However, based on the information in the passage, the effectiveness of bans on texting behind the wheel is not proven.

The following is an example of an **ineffective** response. It needs more development. To practice your writing, try revising and editing this response to improve it.

Texting while driving is a very dangerous activity, and if an activity is dangerous, then we should respond to it with laws. Since 40% of teens have been in cars where the driver did dangerous texting, the problem is widespread. The only evidence shown against bans on texting while driving is one study. A single study does not give a large body of evidence. However, the dangers of texting are extreme, accounting for about one tenth of crashes involving young drivers. Laws against texting while driving protect potentially irresponsible drivers, passing drivers obeying the law, and passengers in both cars. They are important and desirable laws.

3. The following is an example of an **effective** response. It has a strong central idea. It also includes specific information from the passage that is clearly organized. The response has a clear beginning, middle, and ending.

The arguments in the passage that oppose banning large sugared soda are stronger. Although neither argument includes specific data about such bans, the argument opposing bans makes a strong case that bans of large sodas will be ineffective.

Proponents of soda bans focus on the harms of sugar. While the argument includes specific evidence such as the high incidence of obesity among adults and the cost of obesity, that evidence doesn't show that a ban on large soda would be effective. Even if sugared sodas were the only cause of obesity (and not merely the largest source of calories), would banning large-sized drinks improve health? The argument gives no evidence to show that it would.

The opponents of soda bans acknowledge the lack of evidence on the effectiveness of those bans. One specific piece of evidence opponents cite is that 80% of sugared sodas are sold in stores. The people who drink large amounts of soda will likely continue to buy large quantities of soda.

When regulating business is ineffective, it is bad policy. Opponents to soda bans state that a ban does not attack the root of obesity, and this statement is true. It may be more difficult to teach healthy eating habits than to institute regulations and bans. However, the easy route is not always the most effective.

The following is an example of an **ineffective** response. It does not focus on a clear central idea. The language choices could be improved to give this response a more formal tone and more variety in sentence structure and language. To practice your writing, try revising and editing this response to improve it.

The passage has information about stopping restaurants from serving large sugared soda. The people who support banning sodas have a lot of information about the costs of obesity. Obesity is a real problem and cost a good deal of money. The people who oppose banning sodas note that nobody knows the effects of a ban. A lot of soda is available from stores instead of restaurants. It is difficult to know if policies will help or not. The policy to ban sodas tries to make people eat better. This is a good goal, at least.

Practice in Social Studies Writing *page 87*

The Relationship Bridge

Practice It!   *pages 92–95*

1.

Bridge End
Issue: Liberty versus safety
Summary: It is not worth giving up liberty to gain safety.
Context: Revolutionary era

Connection
In her criticism of NSA data collection, Conroy weighs the two conflicting values, liberty and safety, that Franklin compares in the quotation.

Bridge End
Issue: Liberty versus security
Summary: Collecting large amounts of data about U.S. citizens creates the probability of abusing that information. In this case, individual liberty is more important than security.
Context: NSA mass data collection

120

Answers and Explanations

2. You might write:

In her criticism of NSA data collection, Conroy weighs the two conflicting values, liberty and safety, that Franklin compares in the quotation. Conroy suggests that liberty and safety are conflicting values that must be balanced, and echoing Franklin's sentiment, states that liberty should outweigh security in regard to NSA data collection. The goal of an intelligence service such as the NSA is to ensure security. Conroy notes that when there is secrecy, there is often a cost to individual liberty. Some limits on individual liberty are acceptable. A secret court might rule that an intelligence agency can place a wire tap on a phone, for example. Even Franklin qualifies his statement about liberty and safety, comparing giving up "essential" liberty to gain "a little temporary" safety. Conroy recognizes that liberty and security need to be balanced but believes that the massive amounts of data collected by the NSA cross a line. Massive data collection is not an issue that Franklin could have anticipated during Revolutionary times, but it evokes the issue of liberty versus safety that Franklin identified.

3.

Bridge End
Issue: Blind patriotism versus responding to the country's problems
Summary: Supporting your country means keeping it on the right path, not blindly supporting anything your country does.
Context: Senate discussion, 1872

Connection
Antonio Marquez reflects Schurz's sentiment through his desire to enhance government oversight.

Bridge End
Issue: Oversight of police officers
Summary: Video surveillance of police creates oversight that can prevent abuse of power as well as false complaints and violence.
Context: Video cameras integrated into police uniforms

4. You might write:

Carl Schurz said, "My country right or wrong; if right to be kept right; and if wrong to be set right." This sentiment opposes blind patriotism, instead advocating for government oversight to keep the country on the right track. Antonio Marquez reflects Schurz's sentiment through his desire to enhance government oversight. He discusses filming police officers on duty. The main argument in favor of video cameras on police uniforms is to create oversight that can prevent abuse of power. While Marquez also mentions preventing false complaints and violent episodes, he focuses on creating oversight for police in their roles as public servants. If the officers are right, oversight will keep them on the right path. If the officers are wrong, oversight will set them right.

Check Your Skills

pages 96–98

1. The following is an example of an **effective** response. It focuses on and explains the connection between the quotation and the passage.

The Fifth Amendment affirms in the U.S. Constitution the right to remain silent, that no one "shall be compelled in any criminal case to be a witness against himself." In its ruling in Salinas v. Texas, the Supreme Court seems to qualify this right by stating that defendants must explicitly evoke the right to silence, instead of simply remaining silent. Morgan appeals to the Fifth Amendment and to the idea of "inalienable rights." Rights are not awarded by the government. Instead, they are inherent rights that the government recognizes. If this view of rights, it is counterintuitive that a person must declare he or she is using a constitutional right before it takes effect. An inherent right never goes away. It can be recognized, or it can be infringed. When the suspect did not answer a question about his shotgun, he was remaining silent, yet the Supreme Court ruled that he was not using his right to remain silent. Morgan's main point is that the Fifth Amendment right to silence is an inherent right, not one that is switched on and off by a declaration.

The following is an example of an **ineffective** response. It is difficult to follow and does not make a clear connection between the quotation and the passage. To practice your writing, try revising and editing this response to improve it.

The Supreme Court says that silence can be used as a kind of evidence in a court case. The possibility of using silence is a way of showing how the suspect reacts or how they talk with the police. This is something that is observed and then told about in a court during a court case, such as the one that is Salinas v. Texas, the case that the Supreme Court ruled on in June 2013. The person used Miranda rights to remain silent when asked about his shotgun and would it match the shells from the murder. It was a serious crime and the person was then arrested and tried, where it was evidence that he wouldn't answer. This is what the problem is, that not answering was used as part of the court case against him.

2. The following is an example of an **effective** response. It makes a clear connection between the passage and the quotation.

The idea of "tyranny of the majority" refers to the majority overwhelming the rights of minority groups by voting against them. However, creating strangely shaped districts based on demographics to keep one party in power evokes the second part of Baron Acton's quotation: the tyranny of a party that succeeds "by force or fraud." Banner's letter reflects this concern.

Banner notes that democracy depends on the accurate representation of votes. Banner suggests that non-partisan redistricting commissions can draw fair, unbiased district boundaries to prevent a party from conniving to unfairly maintain power. He provides a specific example of such a commission created in California in 2010 to avoid the tyranny of the elected party over district boundaries. More information about the successes of such commissions would better support Banner's position, but the fact that the commission is composed of democrats, republicans, and people associated with neither party reflects Baron Acton's concerns. By implementing this solution nationally, Banner hopes to avoid at least part of Baron Acton's concerns and prevent one way that a party can become a tyrant through democracy.

The following is an example of an **ineffective** response. It lacks focus, is redundant and confusing, and does not make a connections between the quotation and the passage. To practice your writing, try revising and editing this response to improve it.

Districts are a normal part of government that allows people to elect officials that represent their particular areas or states. There is never going to be a district that everyone is happy with because everyone wants a district that might vote for them instead of voting for their competitors. There is no way for it to be fair, and it just depends on who is in power right now. Tomorrow someone else will be in power and make their own district lines. That's why it doesn't make any sense for having politicians declaring their own political lines, but it isn't something that can be helped. Everyone is biased and always someone is doing the wrong thing. When you make a political boundary, you are making political friends and enemies. It's always the politicians that you can't trust, and everyone is biased. There is no way you can be unbiased or really independent, because everyone has their own opinion that they support.

3. The following is an example of an **effective** response. It explains the meaning of Hamilton's quotation and applies the concept to the blog post. It makes a clear connection between the quotation and the passage.

The quotation from Alexander Hamilton advocates for moderation in government, warning against extremes. In the blog post, Olsen discusses the electoral college, which is an attempt to create moderate democracy. The electoral college is a form of representative democracy, similar to Congress. Instead of voting directly, each state sends representatives to the electoral college to vote for president. This gives power to the states. It might be considered an "extreme of democracy" to have individuals vote directly for the president. However, the movement toward a direct presidential vote reflects the changes in the U.S. since Hamilton's time. The federal government is more powerful, and the state governments are less independent. Olsen uses a specific example of how the electoral college changed a presidential election. The reason it seems so strange for the presidential election and the electoral college votes to be different is because we think of the presidential race as a national election, not a decision made between the states. Without strong, independent states, perhaps the more reasonable, moderate choice today would be to eliminate the electoral college. It is no longer an extreme of democracy to vote directly for president.

The following is an example of an **ineffective** response. Its language is confusing, and it does not make a connection between the quotation and the passage. To practice your writing, try revising and editing this response to improve it.

The electoral college is a way to elect the president. It works because it's done by states. It seems like Al Gore got more votes but George W. Bush got more votes in the electoral college. George Bush was elected president. The idea is states have representatives for the electoral college, and really when you vote it goes to vote for the representatives. They say who they vote for in the electoral college. That is what determines who is the next president. It is an extra step in the process of elections that sometimes can go wrong. Most of the time it works fine, though, and it means that each state gets their representation in government. Congress has state representation, too, and this just applies it to the electoral college for presidential elections.

Resources

Use the following resources to continue practicing and improving your writing. Resources for language and grammar can help you avoid mistakes that can hinder communication. Writing prompts can give you extra practice to develop your writing.

The Writing Process, Grammar, and Mechanics

 The Purdue University Online Writing Lab (OWL) has resources covering academic writing, the writing process, and writing grammar and mechanics. Use this resource to improve your language skills.
https://owl.english.purdue.edu/owl/

 HyperGrammar contains information on parts of speech, phrases, clauses, sentences, punctuation, and paragraphs. Find useful references on all aspects of the English language.
http://www.uottawa.ca/academic/arts/writcent/hypergrammar/

Dictionaries

 The Oxford Dictionary website includes definitions, synonyms, grammar references, word origins, games and quizzes, and foreign language dictionaries.
http://www.oxforddictionaries.com/us

 The Merriam-Webster® online dictionary includes a dictionary and thesaurus, as well as quizzes and games, a word-of-the-day feature, and helpful videos about language issues.
http://www.merriam-webster.com/

Common Errors

 Visit the *Common Errors in English Usage* website to explore errors from *a* versus *an* to *your* versus *you're*. In addition to an extensive list of errors, this site has a daily calendar and a blog.
https://public.wsu.edu/~brians/errors/errors.html

 Find common grammar errors and FAQs at GrammarMonster.com. Topics include abbreviations, apostrophes, plurals, comparatives, and many more.
http://www.grammar-monster.com/common_grammar_errors.htm

 "Common Mistakes of English Grammar, Mechanics, and Punctuation" by Dr. Jeffrey Kahn, Illinois State University, provides a brief list of common errors, along with examples of right and wrong usage.
http://my.ilstu.edu/~jhkahn/writing.html

Writing Prompts

 Use these four essay prompts from the most recent SAT® test administration for extra writing practice.
https://professionals.collegeboard.com/testing/sat-reasoning/prep/essay-prompts

 This webpage at the Writing Center at the University of North Carolina at Chapel Hill explains how to interpret academic assignments and writing prompts.
https://writingcenter.unc.edu/handouts/understanding-assignments/

 This list of 100 brief persuasive writing prompts at the Writing Prompts website can help you practice using claims and evidence. When you use these prompts, research your topic to find strong arguments.
http://www.writingprompts.net/persuasive/

Word Processing

 Google® Drive allows you to create online documents. You can use this word processor to practice keyboarding, navigating a written document on a computer, and using features such as cut, copy, and paste.
http://www.google.com/drive/apps.html